Differentiating by Student Learning Preferences:

Strategies and Lesson Plans

Joni Turville

EYE ON EDUCATION
6 DEPOT WAY WEST, SUITE 106
LARCHMONT, NY 10538
(914) 833–0551
(914) 833–0761 fax
www.eyeoneducation.com

Library of Congress Cataloging-in-Publication Data

Turville, Joni.
Differentiating by student learning preferences : strategies and lesson plans / by Joni Turville.
      p. cm.
   Includes bibliographical references and index.
   ISBN 978-1-59667-082-2
1. Individualized instruction. 2. Lesson planning. I. Title.
LB1031.T8742 2008
31.39'4—dc22

                                        2008005293

   10 9 8 7 6 5 4 3 2

Also Available from EYE ON EDUCATION

Differentiating by Student Interest:
Strategies and Lesson Plans
Joni Turville

Differentiated Instruction for K–8 Math and Science:
Ideas, Activities, and Lesson Plans
Mary Hamm and Dennis Adams

Differentiated Instruction:
A Guide for Elementary School Teachers
Amy Benjamin

Differentiated Assessment
for Middle and High School Classrooms
Deborah Blaz

Differentiated Instruction Using Technology:
Guide for Middle and High School Teachers
Amy Benjamin

Handbook on Differentiated Instruction
for Middle and High Schools
Sheryn Northey

The Democratic Differentiated Classroom
Sheryn Waterman

Differentiated Instruction:
A Guide for Middle and High School Teachers
Amy Benjamin

Teacher-Made Assessments:
Connecting Curriculum, Instruction, and Student Learning
Christopher R. Gareis and Leslie W. Grant

Family Reading Night
Darcy Hutchins, Marsha Greenfeld, and Joyce Epstein

Family Math Night:
Math Standards in Action
Jennifer Taylor-Cox

A School for Each Student:
Personalization in a Climate of High Expectations
Nelson Beaudoin

Dedication

For my mom, Adele. You are the wind beneath my wings.

Acknowledgments

My first thanks are to my family, who put up with the crazy pace of my life and who love and support me no matter what. I love you so much. You are my inspiration.

To my peer reviewers: Lois Gluck, Melany Carter, and Peggy Bergmann. Thank you for helping me muck through the rough first draft and for your wise feedback. You are my reality check.

Thanks to the many colleagues who have been instrumental in supporting and encouraging me over the years, particularly the amazingly talented Barb Scott, my friend and colleague with whom I shared a classroom and all of the other parts of my life. I am also grateful for the dedicated staff in my home district, St. Albert Protestant Schools. Special thanks go to Grace Christophers, Joan Trettler, Gloria Gogowich, Mary Stoker, Joe Demko, Barry Wowk, Michele Dick, Robert Hogg, Rosemary Foster, and the other instructional leaders who helped me believe that I could be a leader, too, and provided me with opportunities along the way. You are my encouragers.

My continued appreciation goes to the wonderful people at Eye On Education, particularly Bob Sickles, who encouraged me to continue this series of books. Thanks to all the editors and layout artists as well. You are my quality control.

I am also indebted to the writers, speakers, and researchers—past, present, and future—who have uncovered and will continue to uncover what we know about differentiated instruction. Even though this work has been around for many years, there is still much more to learn. You are my grounding.

Finally, my great admiration goes to the classroom teachers who work with students every day. You are the people who take the theories, musings, and ideas of many people and bring them to life in order to help students learn. You are my heroes.

Meet the Author

Joni Turville is the Coordinator for the Alberta Initiative School Improvement program in St. Albert, Alberta, Canada. She has taught a wide range of subjects, including special education and technology, at the elementary, secondary, and university levels. For the past several years she has worked in district administration, working with K–12 teachers. Joni has also been involved in consulting on various topics, particularly educational technology and differentiated instruction. She frequently presents nationally and internationally.

Free Downloads

Beginning on page 101, you'll find 57 Blackline Masters. Book buyers have permission to print out these Adobe Acrobat © documents and duplicate them to distribute to your students.

You can access these downloads by visiting Eye On Education's website: www.eyeoneducation.com. Click on FREE Downloads or search or browse our website to find this book and then scroll down for downloading instructions.

You'll need your book-buyer access code: **DIFFST-7082-2**

Table of Contents

1
Differentiating by Learning Preferences

The biggest mistake of past centuries in teaching has been to treat all children as if they were variants of the same individual.

—Howard Gardner

I give credit for much of my learning success to my seventh-grade language arts teacher, Mr. Buccini. Early in the year, he had a discussion about studying for an upcoming quiz and talked about different ways to study. As he was talking, I was thinking about how I liked to learn. I thought that rather than just reading my notes over and over, I would tape-record them and listen to them instead. This studying technique worked so well that I have used it ever since.

From my own personal experiences as a learner and from watching students in the classroom, I became interested in examining and using learning preferences to improve learning. When I first heard the term *differentiated instruction* used and described, I thought to myself, "Hey, I do that!" I know that as you read this book, you will have many of those moments, too. This book will offer a variety of ways to think about differentiating instruction by learning preferences.

A Step Back:
What Is Differentiated Instruction?

Through our experiences with people of all ages, we can say with confidence that people differ in the ways in which they learn. This is very apparent in a classroom, where a teacher is responsible for ensuring that subject-matter outcomes are met while dealing with an extremely diverse group of students. Differentiated instruction provides a way of thinking about teaching and learning that helps teachers not only recognize differences but also offers a framework in which to respond.

One model that is often used in planning for differentiated instruction is one that was conceptualized by Carol Ann Tomlinson of the University of Virginia (Figure 1.1). It is certainly not the only model or the only way to think about differentiated instruction; however, it is used and well accepted by many educators. The graphic makes it quite easy to see the different components and how they are interrelated.

Tomlinson (2001) says that teachers can differentiate three things: the content, which is the *what* of teaching; the process, or the *how* of teaching; and the product, which is how students *demonstrate understanding* of their learning. In order to determine what to differentiate, teachers must first determine how *ready* students are for a particular concept, what their *interests* are, and what their *learning profile* is.

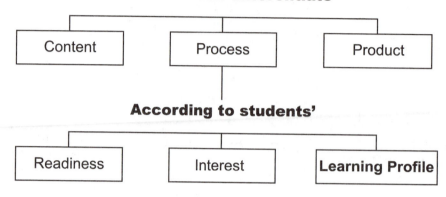

**Figure 1.1. Differentiated Instruction Model
(Tomlinson 2001)**

Teachers can differentiate

| Content | Process | Product |

According to students'

| Readiness | Interest | Learning Profile |

This Book Series

This series of books has been designed to help teachers focus on one particular aspect of differentiation at a time. The components of differentiated instruction cannot be completely separated from each another, but by exploring in depth, teachers may be able to get a picture of what differentiation might look like in the classroom without being overwhelmed. The three books, one focusing on student interest, one on readiness, and this one on learning profiles, are all interrelated, and they can give teachers practical strategies and lesson plans in each area so that they can study and adapt for their particular group of learners, and together they can help teachers develop a comprehensive view of differentiation.

What Are Learning Preferences?

Tomlinson defines a *learning profile* as a composite of the "ways in which we learn best as individuals" (2001, p. 60). It can include things such as learning styles, personality styles, culture, gender, intelligences, and learning environment preferences. These terms have been used and interpreted differently in literature. In this book, the term *learning preference* will be used in a broad sense to include student learning styles, intelligences and preferences, and other factors that influence how students respond to learning experiences. Moving beyond the definitions and theories, the purpose of this book is to present practical ways to recognize and celebrate differences and to provide a variety of experiences that can positively influence students. It is a hopeful way of thinking—it recognizes that students are different, but that we can use their strengths for personal development and to accomplish meaningful learning.

Research Connections

Learning can be described as a highly personal process in which each person absorbs and retains information and skills (Dunn, 1984; Teele, 1999; Williamson & Watson, 2006). Sparks and Castro (2006) write of a necessary paradigm shift from learning new information to understanding the process of learning itself. Helping students discover how they learn best and using this information to their advantage can help them to "learn how to learn" for a lifetime.

Thomas Armstrong, in his book *Multiple Intelligences in the Classroom* (2000, p. 17), describes some of the factors that can affect the ways in which we learn. They include biology (including heredity, genetic factors, and brain injuries), personal experiences (including interactions with parents, teachers, friends, and other people of significance and access to resources) and culture or history (including time and place of birth and cultural influences).

Learning Preferences Are Not Stagnant

A frequent misconception about learning preferences is that they are set early in life and never change. In fact, they develop over time with our previous and continuous experiences (Armstrong, 2004; Silver, Strong & Perini, 1997; Sparks & Castro, 2006; Sternberg & Grigorenko, 2004; Sternberg & Zhang, 2005). Some key ideas include the following:

♦ Our preferences are not "good" or "bad"; rather, what may influence the experience is the fit between the student and the material or the student and the method of learning.

♦ The way in which we respond can vary across tasks and situations.

♦ People differ in the strength of their preferences. Some people prefer certain styles very strongly, whereas others have weaker preferences.

♦ Some learners can switch easily between different ways of learning and others cannot (Sternberg & Zhang, 2005, pp. 245–246).

It is important to share these key ideas with students so that they are encouraged to experiment with different kinds of tasks, which will help them develop different ways of learning. They must also understand that learning preference does not equal ability.

Students Have the Capacity
to Develop Balance in Learning Preferences

People do not have just one type of learning preference. Often they have several types that work well for them. In fact, some learners have a degree of balance between learning preferences, and many everyday tasks require different kinds of thinking at the same time. Most people are not equally adept in all areas, but greater balance can be developed over time (Sternberg, 2000; Williamson & Watson, 2006). It is not important to label students as certain kinds of learners but rather to help them work toward balance. When working on unfamiliar and challenging tasks, or when learners are feeling discouraged, it is certainly beneficial to have them to work in their areas of strength. They need to work in different ways over time so that they can work in ways that feel comfortable, as well as in less comfortable ways that challenge them to develop as learners (McCarthy, 1985).

Is There an Impact on Student Achievement?

Teaching using student learning preferences can seem complex; it is important for teachers to be confident that their efforts will make a difference for students. Over the years, there have been a number of studies that support the idea that teaching using learning preferences can positively influence learning (Gardner, 1999; Geimer, Getz, Pochert & Pullam, 2000; Gens, Provance, VanDuyne, & Zimmerman, 1998; Greenhawk, 1997; Kuzniewski, Sanders, Smith, Swanson, & Urich, 1998; Mettetal, Jordan, & Harper, 1997). Research has shown that regardless of how they are assessed, students who are taught in a way that is a better fit with their preferences outperform students who are taught in a way that is a mismatch for them. In other words, "[T]hey outperform students instructed in conventional ways, even if the assessments are for straight factual memory" (Sternberg & Zhang, 2005). There is some thought that teaching in areas of strength encourages deeper, more elaborate, and more diverse encoding of material than does learning in less preferred modes. Teaching in this way can enhance the probability of retrieval of important information at test time (Sternberg & Grigorenko, 2004).

Learning Preference Models

Learning style theory goes back to Carl Jung (1927), who noted observed differences in the way people perceived information, the way they made decisions, and how active or reflective they were. Over the years, many researchers have developed theories to describe differences in approaches to learning. This book will focus on lesson planning using three different models of learning preferences: the visual auditory kinesthetic model, the multiple intelligences model (conceived by Howard Gardner), and the triarchic intelligences model (developed by Robert Sternberg). Teachers should examine each model and decide which fits best with their own understanding, philosophy, and capacity for planning instruction.

Visual Auditory Kinesthetic Model

This model is often referred to as the "learning styles" model (Van Klaveren et al., 2002) and has been used in many different ways over a long period of time. When working with teachers on incorporating learning preference choices, this may be a good place to begin, as the concepts of visual, auditory, and kinesthetic learners will likely be familiar (Figure 1.2). Learning style can be referred to as a "distinctive and habitual manner of acquiring knowledge, skills or attitudes through study or experience" (Smith & Dalton, 2005).

Figure 1.2. Visual Auditory Kinesthetic Model

Visual learners. . . . . Learn by viewing
Auditory learners . . . . Learn by hearing and speaking
Kinesthetic learners. . . . . Learn through hands on and movement

It is thought that when students understand their own learning styles, they can make informed choices about what works for their learning, and teachers can use this information to plan for student success.

Multiple Intelligences Model

Harvard cognitive psychologist Howard Gardner introduced the theory of multiple intelligences in his book *Frames of Mind* (1983). He examined the findings of hundreds of studies from disciplines such as cognitive and developmental psychology, differential psychology, neurosciences, anthropology, and cultural studies. One of the interesting things that Gardner proposed was a reframing of the word "intelligence." The concept that there are many ways to be "smart" can have a powerful impact on how teachers see their students and plan instruction. Gardner defines intelligence as the potential to process information to solve problems and to create products that are of value (Gardner & Moran, 2006). Gardner proposes eight intelligences that he has researched and identified (Figure 1.3).

Figure 1.3. Multiple Intelligences Model

Verbal/linguistic...	Thinks in words and uses language well
Logical/mathematical...	Thinks logically and uses numbers well
Visual/spatial...	Thinks visually and uses pictures and designs well
Musical/rhythmic...	Thinks musically and uses rhythm and melodies well
Body/kinesthetic...	Thinks through touching and movement and uses the body well
Naturalist...	Thinks through nature and uses categorization and natural events well
Interpersonal...	Thinks through interactions with others and cooperates well
Intrapersonal...	Thinks through reflection and uses self-awareness and feelings well

Gardner has also identified a possible ninth intelligence, "existentialist," but he "is not yet convinced if fulfils the criteria" of an intelligence (Gardner & Moran, 2006). Gardner is continually assessing and refining multiple intelligences theory.

Triarchic Intelligences Model

Conceptualized by a professor of psychology and education at Yale University, Robert Sternberg (2000), the triarchic intelligences model outlines three intelligences that people possess (Figure 1.4).

Figure 1.4. Triarchic Intelligences Model

Analytical...	The ability to analyze and evaluate ideas
Practical...	The ability to convince people of the value of ideas and to make the ideas of practical value
Creative...	The ability to easily generate one or more ideas that are novel and of high quality

Sternberg emphasizes that no one fits purely into one category and that there is a need for balance. He goes on to say, "the triarchic theory is not just an armchair classification of abilities. It is supported by empirical research on thousands of participants of various ages from many countries, using a variety of different methodologies" (Sternberg, 2000, p. 234).

Words of Caution

Using learning preferences as a model for planning instruction can help to differentiate, but it is only one way to consider differentiating instruction. Gardner (1999) has never advocated a recipe for implementing his ideas on multiple intelligences. He cautions against superficial application and instead focuses on three ideas:

> We are not all the same; we do not have all the same kinds of minds (that is, we are not all distinct points on a single bell curve); and education works most effectively if these differences are taken into account rather than denied or ignored. Taking human differences seriously lies at the heart of the MI [multiple intelligences] perspective. At the theoretical level, this means that all individuals cannot be profitably arrayed on a single intellectual dimension. At the practical level, it suggests that any uniform educational approach is likely to serve only a small percentage of children optimally. (Gardner, 1999, p. 91)

No matter which model we use, we must not simply label students according to their strengths and then carry on teaching the same way we have always done. We must be prepared to respond and help students develop effective ways to learn. By choosing a framework for differentiating and using specific models of learning preferences, we can begin to understand the diversity of our students and incorporate specific techniques in order to help students learn.

Tying Things Together

This chapter has provided background information on differentiated instruction and learning preferences. Some of the research that supports teaching through learning preferences has also been synthesized. Chapter 2 will discuss ways in which teachers can assess the learning preferences of students and build a classroom climate that supports differentiation.

For Further Reflection

♦ Which models of differentiated instruction do I currently use to plan for instruction? How do they work to help me differentiate in a systematic way?

♦ How does the research reflect my experiences with students?

♦ What personal learning experiences have I had that would demonstrate a link between learning preferences and achievement?

2

Assessing Learning Preferences and Building Classroom Climate

Treat people as if they were what they ought to be, and you can help them become what they are capable of becoming.

—Johann Wolfgang von Goethe

There are many formal and informal ways to assess the learning preferences of students. This chapter presents some of the ways you can gather this information. As students do these activities, it is important to emphasize that preferences are not static—they change over time. It is also possible to purposely develop strength in different areas. A second focus of this chapter is to share ideas to help build a classroom climate that supports differentiation. In order for learning to take place, students must feel that they are in a safe environment where their uniqueness will be respected, so it is important to not only assess but also celebrate the individuality of each student.

Assessing Learning Preferences

Students who are very verbal and confident will often talk about themselves, what works for them, and how they spend their time outside school. Other students, however, will be reluctant to share information about themselves. Using a variety of formal and informal learning preference assessments can help teachers get to know all their students, including those who are hesitant to share (Figure 2.1). This information can then be used to plan effective learning experiences to meet a range of learner needs and preferences.

Technology Connection

An Internet search using search terms such as "learning style inventory" or "multiple intelligences survey" will yield a number of inventories that teachers can use if they would like to extend the ideas presented in the blackline masters. If you want to search for the exact term, type the phrase surrounded by quotation marks (e.g., "learning styles survey" rather than learning styles survey).

Figure 2.1. Student Inventory

Name_____Date_____

Circle the face that best describes how you feel about the following statements.

1. I like working with others.

2. I like to do jigsaw puzzles and mazes.

3. I like quiet places.

4. I like sports.

5. I like music.

6. I like playing alone.

Learning Preferences Inventories

Inventories can be an effective tool for assessing the ways in which students learn. They can be completed independently by students who are able to read and write well. For students who having difficulty completing them independently, these supports could also be used:

♦ Cross-age partners

♦ Parent volunteer readers and scribes

♦ Tape-recorded responses

♦ Drawn responses with scribed descriptions

Samples of inventories that can be used by a variety of students can be found in the Blackline Masters section at the end of this book. There is a primary inventory for younger students (Blackline Master 1, pp. 102-103) and versions for older students (Blackline Master 2, p. 104).

Assessing Learning Preferences in Young Children

A variety of inventories exist for young children; however, children at this age often have difficulty describing what kinds of learning work best for them. In fact, many teachers prefer not to use formal assessments with young students but rather provide a wide variety of activities and observe which ones students gravitate toward and those at which they succeed. Some teachers have found that the Teele Inventory for Multiple Intelligences Inventory gives useful results, as it has children make a choice between two "panda bears." Ordering information for this resource can be found at http://www.sueteele.com.

Visual Auditory Kinesthetic Inventory (Blackline Master 3)

Students who are a little older likely have a sense of which kinds of learning work for them when they are prompted with some descriptors. In order to conduct this type of informal inventory, the teacher reads aloud a series of descriptors, and the students rate themselves on a scale of 1 to 10, where 1 means that the description isn't very much like them and 10 means that the description is exactly like them. Students can shade in the number of boxes to indicate their visual auditory kinesthetic preferences to create a bar graph (Figure 2.2). This is not a formal inventory but rather a tool to help students become more aware of their strengths.

Figure 2.2. Visual Auditory Kinesthetic Inventory Sample

Visual	*Auditory*	*Kinesthetic*

Multiple Intelligences Inventory
(Blackline Master 4)

An informal multiple intelligences inventory can be done in the same way as the visual auditory kinesthetic inventory, except the teacher reads a descriptor of eight multiple intelligences while students use a scale of 1 to 10 to determine how much each intelligence describes themselves. Students shade in boxes to create a bar graph that represents their intelligences strengths. This informal tool is designed to help students learn about multiple intelligences, to begin to think about their own areas of strength, and to develop a common vocabulary that can be used in the classroom.

Triarchic Intelligences Inventory
(Blackline Master 5)

An informal triarchic intelligences inventory can be done in the same way as the previous two inventories. The teacher reads descriptors of the three intelligences while students use a scale of 1 to 10 to determine how much each intelligence describes themselves. Boxes are shaded in to create a bar graph that represents their strengths. This inventory is designed to help students learn about triarchic intelligences, to begin to think about their own areas of strength, and to develop a common vocabulary that can be used in the classroom.

Parent-Completed Questionnaires

Remember to use parents as a resource to find out more about student learning preferences. Studies have shown the positive impact of parent involvement on student success at school (Nakagawa, 2000; Mattingly, Prislin, McKenzie, Rodriguez, & Kayzar, 2002). They are the experts on their children and will be able to provide important information through such inventories (Figure 2.3). Blackline Masters 6 and 7 contain two versions of questionnaires for use with parents.

If you are teaching using learning preferences schoolwide, you might also consider having a parent evening at which parents learn about different intelligences and complete an inventory themselves. Some interesting discussions can occur as parents reflect on their own learning preferences and how they are similar to or different from their child's. This may also give parents insight into how to help their children study more effectively at home.

Technology Connection

Online surveys can be used to collect information quickly and easily. There are a variety of sites with such tools available, such as http://formsite.com, http://surveymonkey.com and http://zoomerang.com. They enable online surveys to be created quickly, without any special computer expertise. The benefit of using them is that students can work through them in a computer lab or on a classroom computer, and the teacher will have instant, tabulated results.

Figure 2.3. Sample Parent Questionnaire

Dear Parents,

The purpose of this inventory is to give information about some of your child's learning preferences so that we can capitalize on them over the course of the school year.

Thank you for completing this survey. Please return to school by _____.

Yours truly,

_____

What kinds of activities does your child gravitate toward? Check all that apply:

❑ Verbal   ❑ Logical/Mathematical

❑ Music   ❑ Physical Activities

❑ Activities in Nature   ❑ Puzzles/Mazes/Drawing

❑ Working Alone   ❑ Working with Others

1. What are your child's favorite subjects in school?

2. What subjects are your child's least favorite?

3. What are your child's interests outside of school?

5. When your child has free time, what does he or she choose to do?

6. What kinds of careers has your child expressed an interest in?

8. Describe how your child learns best (in a quiet place, with others, talking, etc.)

9. What else can you tell me about the way your child learns best?

10. What two words best describe how your child learns?

Other Activities to Learn about and Celebrate Unique Learning Preferences

Learning Preferences Posters

Using the model you have chosen, find poster-sized pieces of paper, suitable for display in the classroom. Have students work in groups to make a heading for each intelligence and draw pictures that represent each way of learning. Create a space where students can sign their names under the intelligences in which they feel they have strengths. These posters can then be used for students to check to see who they might be able to ask for help with a particular kind of task. Alternatively, there are learning preferences posters (Figure 2.4) available in the Blackline Master section at the end of this book if you prefer to enlarge them and display ready-made posters (Blackline Masters 8–21).

Figure 2.4. Sample Learning Preferences Posters

Learning Preferences People Search

Students can get to know the strengths of their classmates and get to know one another by participating in a "learning preferences people search" (Figure 2.5) at the beginning of the year. They could keep the completed people search forms in a folder or binder and use the information to find classmates who can help them if they need assistance with a task (Blackline Master 22).

Figure 2.5. Learning Preferences People Search

Name: _____

Move around the classroom and have classmates sign their names in one of the squares that describes them.

Likes to draw	Remembers math facts	Plays a sport	Enjoys reading
Can remember a poem	Keeps a diary	Enjoys working in groups	Likes plants and animals
Likes doing crafts	Plays an instrument	Likes solving problems	Can interpret a graph
Enjoys being outside	Enjoys working alone	Can read a map	Enjoys taking things apart and putting things together
Likes to write	Enjoys jigsaw puzzles	Enjoys listening to music	Enjoys helping others

How I Use My Learning Preferences

Students are given a handout that lists the intelligences from the model being used (Blackline Masters 23–25, pp. 129-131). In each square, they are to draw or write words to represent all of the ways that each learning preference could be used (Figure 2.6). They could place a check mark beside the intelligence that they believe is their strongest and put a star beside the one they would most like to develop during the school year. These could also be stored in a binder or folder and added to throughout the school year as students reflect on how their learning preferences have changed.

Figure 2.6. How I Use My Visual Auditory Kinesthetic Preferences

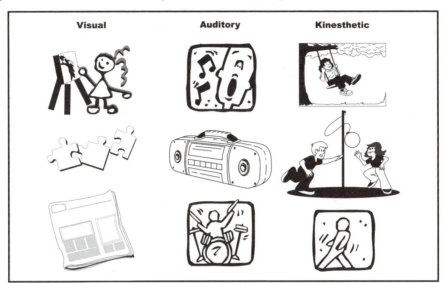

Classroom Learning Preferences Quilt

As a class, discuss learning preferences. The teacher may wish to read a story such as *Ish*, by Peter Reynolds, as a warm-up activity. Students can do a think/pair/share to talk about their personal preferences and talents. Each student is then given a quilt square, either paper or fabric, and uses markers to draw items that represent his or her learning preferences. Students can add words beneath such as "I am body smart" (Figure 2.7). A blank patchwork quilt square can be found on Blackline Master 26 (p. 132).

Figure 2.7. Learning Preferences Quilt Square

Brittany

I am visual smart, self smart, number smart, music smart, and body smart!

Learning Preferences Venn Diagram Interviews

This activity will allow pairs of students to get to know each other and compare their learning preferences. Students interview each other in pairs to discuss their individual learning preferences. This can be done after individual inventories have been completed. They create a large Venn diagram together (Figure 2.8) to share and post as part of a classroom display. A blank Venn diagram can be found on Blackline Master 27. A triple Venn diagram could be used to make the task more challenging (Blackline Master 28, p. 134).

Figure 2.8. Venn Diagram Interview Sample

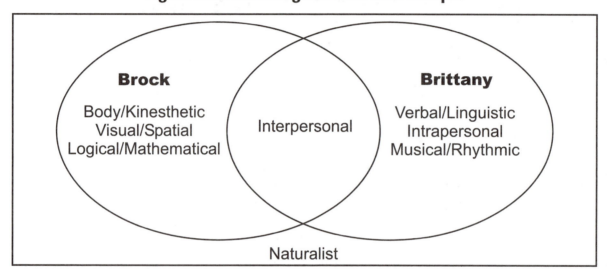

Learning Preferences Graphing

In small groups, students discuss their learning preferences using the model the teacher has chosen (visual auditory kinesthetic, multiple intelligences, or triarchic intelligences). They share their preferred ways of learning and create a tally as they talk and then create a graph of their group's preferences (Figure 2.9). They could use a bar graph, pictograph, or computer-generated graph. A whole-class graph could also be created as a display of learning strengths in the classroom. Graphs for each of the three intelligence models can be found on Blackline Masters 29–30 (pp. 135-136).

Figure 2.9. Sample Learning Preferences Graph

Analytical	Practical	Creative

Technology Connection

Teachers can have students use a spreadsheet or graphing program to create an electronic graph. It can then be manipulated into a variety of formats, such as a pie graph or line graph. If you have an interactive white board in your school, you could consider importing the data into a single spreadsheet and then manipulating the data display to demonstrate and graph the entire class.

Recordkeeping

Once inventories and observations are complete, teachers must find a way to capture this information so that a clear picture of each child can be developed. These records can be kept on something as simple as an index card or on a more detailed student preference sheet (Figures 2.10 and 2.11) can be used. An example of this type tracking form can be found n Blackline Masters 32–35 (pp. 138-141).

Figure 2.10. Student Learning Preference Sheet

Student name: _____ Grade: _____

Readiness
Circle the descriptor most applicable:

Reading	Below Grade Level	At Grade Level	Above Grade Level
Writing	Below Grade Level	At Grade Level	Above Grade Level
Math	Below Grade Level	At Grade Level	Above Grade Level
Science	Below Grade Level	At Grade Level	Above Grade Level
Social Studies	Below Grade Level	At Grade Level	Above Grade Level

Learning Preferences
Circle as many as are applicable:

Sternberg:

Analytical	Practical	Creative

Gardner:

Verbal/ Linguistic	Logical/ Mathematical	Visual/ Spatial	Body/ Kinesthetic
Naturalist	Musical/ Rhythmic	Interpersonal	Intrapersonal

Visual Auditory Kinesthetic:

Visual	Auditory	Kinesthetic

Interests

Other (group/individual orientation, parent observations, etc.):

Figure 2.11. Triarchic Classroom Tracking Form

Check all of the intelligences strengths that apply to each student in the corresponding columns.

Student Name	Analytical	Practical	Creative
Classroom Profile Totals			

Tying Things Together

This chapter has described strategies to assess learning preferences and activities that can be used to recognize and celebrate learning preferences. Taking time to talk about learning strengths is an important component of developing classroom climate, and it is the first step on the road to differentiation. Remember to participate in these activities yourself! A teacher self-reflection tool (Figure 2.12) is provided on Blackline Master 36 (p. 142). By sharing your own learning strengths and how they have evolved over the years, students can get to know you and understand that even adults have areas in which they are confident and others they are working toward improvement.

Figure 2.12. Teacher Self-Reflection Tool

Teacher Learning Preferences Self-Reflection

This self-reflection tool is designed to help you think about your own learning strengths, how they have changed over time, and what the implications are for teaching and learning with your students.

1. My learning profile strengths are:

2. My intelligences have developed over the years in the following ways:

3. The ways my own profiles affect my teaching are:

4. Intelligences I want to more consciously incorporate:

For Further Reflection

♦ What are my current practices for assessing learning preferences and creating a positive, accepting classroom climate?

♦ How will I add new activities or adapt existing ones to continue to create a climate that supports differentiation?

♦ How will I continue to recognize and celebrate differences throughout the school year?

♦ How do my own learning preferences influence the way I teach?

3

Activity Structures That Support Differentiation by Learning Preference

If what we teach diminishes who we teach and erodes how we teach, we are no longer teaching.

Carol Ann Tomlinson

There are different activity structures that can be used to help differentiate by learning preferences. Examples of such structures are choice boards, RAFTs, cubing activities, learning contracts, and WebQuests. This chapter will describe each of these activities and provide step-by-step instructions for creating them.

Being Specific with Learning Outcomes

The first step in using these activity structures (and in creating any differentiated lesson) is to make explicit what students should *know, understand,* and be able to *do* as a result of the lesson. Diane Heacox (2002) refers to this as "KUDos." If you are not completely clear on what students should be learning, they may not end up learning the important outcomes or standards. The types of activity structures described in this chapter may take longer than a single class, so the teacher must also decide whether these activities are worth the students' time and effort.

Understanding KUDos

There can be confusion when trying to specify learning outcomes, especially distinguishing between the "know" and "understand." Using the graphic of an apple (Figure 3.1), these concepts may be more easily understood.

Figure 3.1. Graphic Representation of KUDos

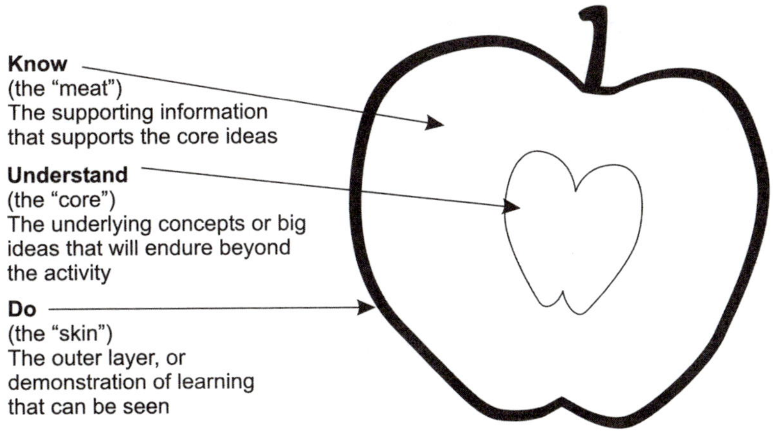

Know
(the "meat")
The supporting information
that supports the core ideas

Understand
(the "core")
The underlying concepts or big
ideas that will endure beyond
the activity

Do
(the "skin")
The outer layer, or
demonstration of learning
that can be seen

The first place to look when beginning to identify KUDos is the required curriculum documents. You want to be sure that no matter what task students do, they will all come to the same knowledge and understanding. These documents typically have a variety of outcome statements, and teachers often must clarify them or break them down into smaller chunks.

A blackline master that contains the apple graphic and descriptions can be found on Blackline Master 37 (p. 143), and it may serve as a quick reference during lesson planning.

Choice Boards

Choice boards are a way of providing students choice within carefully selected tasks. These tasks can be placed on a poster board or chart, or they can be provided on a student handout or overhead. Choice boards can take the form of a tic-tac-toe game board or simply be a list of options. Giving students choices in their learning enhances student engagement and increases the opportunities for student success. Researchers have found that allowing choice can create a high level of interest and motivation (Collins & Amabile, 1999).

Choice boards can be used in any subject area, and be differentiated in a number of ways. They can facilitate the demonstration of knowledge and understanding of a topic or concept (Figure 3.2).

Figure 3.2. Story Response Choice Board (Triarchic)

Analytical	Listen to or read a story and create a chart that tells about the theme or message of the story.
Practical	Think of a time when you or someone you know was in a situation similar to the main character in the story. Draw and/or write about it and include the theme or message that was similar to the story.
Creative	Imagine that the story continues after the last page. Write or act out the next scene. This scene should relate to the theme or message of the story.

Steps to Create a Choice Board

1. Use curriculum documents to determine what you want the students to know, understand, and be able to do (KUDos).

2. Brainstorm a variety of tasks based on what you know about the learning preferences of your students.

3. Eliminate tasks that will not lead the students to KUDos.

4. Decide on the structure of your board. Will you create a tic-tac-toe, a list of choices, or something else?

5. Choose the activities from your brainstormed list and place them on the choice board.

6. Determine how student work will be shared and assessed.

A graphic of these steps can be found on Blackline Master 38 (p. 144).

RAFTs

The acronym RAFT stands for *role, audience, format,* and *topic.* It was originally used as a strategy to help students write from different perspectives, but in recent years, it has been adopted by those who are interested in differentiated instruction and can involve the creation of products beyond only writing. RAFTs help to differentiate because they can provide learning preference choices for students and can be written so that the choices are particularly engaging and targeted to learning preferences. Figure 3.3 provides an explanation of each component of a RAFT, and an example follows in Figure 3.4.

Figure 3.3. RAFT Components

	Role	*Audience*	*Format*	*Topic*
What it is	Students assume a role that is related in some manner to the task.	Students create the product for an identified person, group, object, etc.	Students create a product that will be used to explain the topic to the audience.	The subject or often the title of the piece of work.
Examples	◆ self ◆ character ◆ real-world worker ◆ historical characters ◆ expert ◆ reporter ◆ inanimate object	◆ self ◆ classmates ◆ media ◆ animals ◆ family members ◆ jury ◆ government body ◆ inanimate objects	◆ song ◆ rap ◆ diary entry ◆ letter ◆ chart ◆ flowchart ◆ poem ◆ map ◆ story ◆ model ◆ dramatization	◆ an attention-grabbing or humorous topic related to the role and audience

Figure 3.4. Parts of Speech RAFT

Role	Audience	Format	Topic
Noun	Jury	Mock trial argument	Reasons why I think I'm the most important part of speech of all.
Verb	Other parts of speech	Invitation	I'm where all the action is!
Adjective	Dear Abby	Letter to an advice column (and response).	I'm always helping out my friend, the noun.
Adverb	Other parts of speech	Lament	Why doesn't anyone ever remember what I do?
Pronoun	Other parts of speech	Cartoon strip	I feel like all I ever do is disguise myself as someone else.
Conjunction	Students	Song or rap	I bring things together.
Preposition	Students	Skit	I make relationships between parts of speech happen!

Tips for Creating RAFTS

♦ You can leave one or more of the components (role, audience, format, or topic) static.

♦ To give students more choice in representing their learning, consider more alternatives for the format, based on their learning preferences.

♦ Consider involving students in creating RAFTs once they are familiar with them.

Steps to Create a RAFT Project

1. Use curriculum documents to determine what you want the students to know, understand, and be able to do (KUDos).

2. Brainstorm a variety of projects based on what you know about the learning preferences of your students (these will become the formats).

3. Brainstorm roles, audiences, and topics for each format.

4. Eliminate ideas that will not lead the students to KUDos.

5. Place the roles, audience formats, and topics into the RAFT.

6. Determine how student work will be shared and assessed.

A graphic of these steps can be found on Blackline Master 39 (p. 145).

Cubing

A cubing activity involves creating a three-dimensional cube. Each face on the cube describes an activity that students must complete in order to achieve their learning goals. The activities on a cube can be generic, based on the learning preference model you are using (Figure 3.5). Blackline Masters 40–42 (pp. 146-148) have generic cubes based on the visual auditory kinesthetic, multiple intelligences, and triarchic models. Cubes can also be specific to the topic at hand (Figure 3.6). They are often used at the end of a unit of study when students have a common language and understanding of a topic. Cubing can create interest because of the elements of novelty and chance. It may be best used once students have had success in working in areas of strength, as there is a chance that they may "roll" a task that isn't compatible with their learning preference. In this way, the manner in which a task is done may provide an extra challenge. It is also possible to create more choice by allowing students to roll the cube twice and choose the task that appeals to them the most.

Alternative Suggestions for Making Cubes

If creating the cubes from paper patterns isn't appealing, try these ideas:

- Put six numbered choices on a chart and roll a regular die to determine the students' project.
- Buy an inexpensive plastic photo cube and insert tasks into the photo places. Roll on a carpet.
- Buy a large, spongy cube or die. Write tasks on laminated task cards and tape to the die.

Steps to Create a Cubing Project

1. Use curriculum documents to determine what you want the students to know, understand, and be able to do (KUDos).

2. Brainstorm a variety of tasks based on what you know about the learning preferences of your students.

3. Eliminate tasks that will not lead the students to KUDos.

4. Choose the best six activities, so that there is one for each face of the cube.

5. Create the cube(s) (a blank cube can be found on Blackline Master 43).

6. Determine how student work will be shared and assessed.

A graphic of this checklist can be found on Blackline Master 44 (p. 150).

Figure 3.5. Triarchic Cube

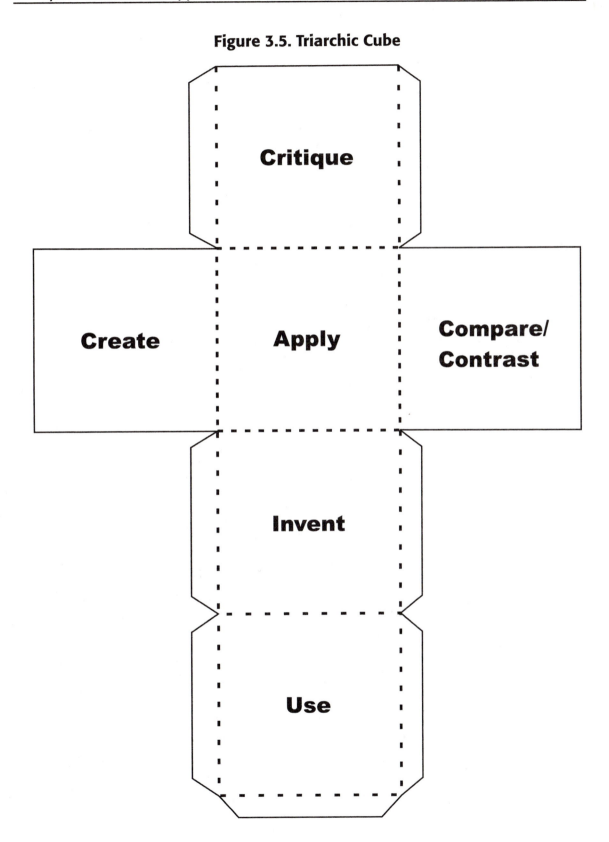

Figure 3.6. Topic-Specific Cube

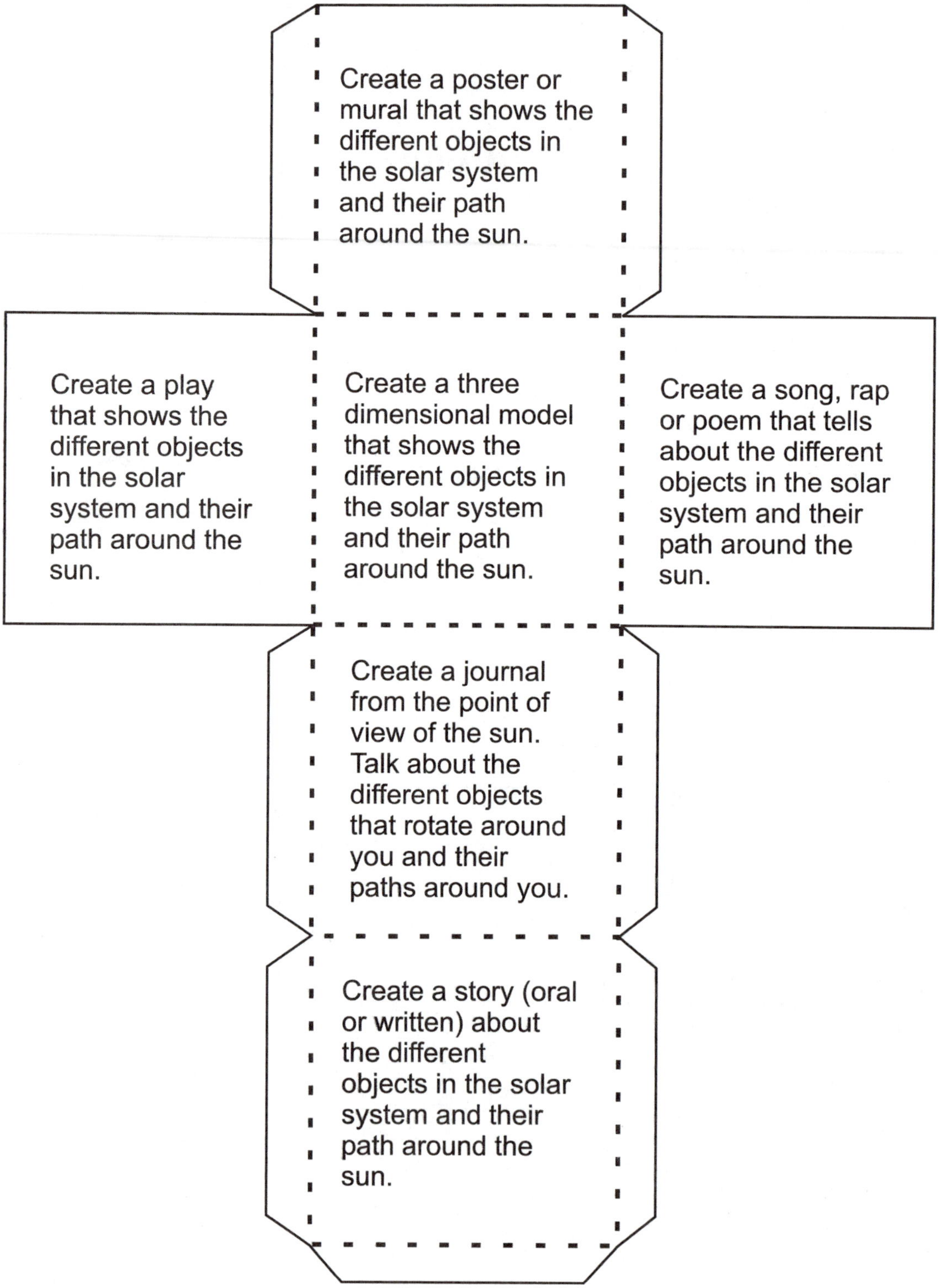

Create a poster or mural that shows the different objects in the solar system and their path around the sun.

Create a play that shows the different objects in the solar system and their path around the sun.

Create a three dimensional model that shows the different objects in the solar system and their path around the sun.

Create a song, rap or poem that tells about the different objects in the solar system and their path around the sun.

Create a journal from the point of view of the sun. Talk about the different objects that rotate around you and their paths around you.

Create a story (oral or written) about the different objects in the solar system and their path around the sun.

Learning Contracts

Learning contracts can be used to allow choice within a range of carefully chosen activities. They are agreements between the teacher and the learner to complete a series of tasks that are designed to achieve specific learning goals. They can be created so that students work individually on an independent study project, in a small group, or as a whole class. They may be developed by the teacher or jointly by the teacher and the students. Most contracts include a place for the date and signatures of the teacher, student, and parents (if desired). This makes it feel like an official contract for the students and signifies that they understand what is required.

Contracts are beneficial because learners are able to make choices, and the teacher is able to bring in different ways of learning, based on what is known about the learning preferences of each group of students. They encourage the development of responsibility and time management skills. Students make choices and complete the tasks they have chosen by the agreed-upon deadline. An example follows.

Figure 3.7. Understanding Characters Learning Contract

Activity 1: Visual

Create a chart that shows how words and actions create a story character.

Activity 2: Auditory

Create an oral editorial that describes how words and acgions create a story character.

Acitivity 3: Kinesthetic

Create tableaus of various story events to show how words and actions create a story character.

Activity Chosen

My activity will be complete and handed in by: _____

Student signature: _____

Teacher signature: _____

Steps to Create a Learning Contract

1. Use curriculum documents to determine what you want the students to know, understand, and be able to do (KUDos).

2. Brainstorm a variety of tasks based on what you know about the learning preferences of your students.

3. Eliminate tasks that will not lead the students to KUDos.

4. Choose activities that will be included in the learning contract.

5. Determine how many tasks students will do.

6. Decide on a reasonable timeline to complete the tasks.

7. Determine in what way and how often you will check in with students during their contract work. Make this explicit in the contract.

8. Outline how students will ask for help, if needed.

9. List the resources that students are able to use and how they should be cited.

10. Write up the contract in a businesslike manner. Include places for dates and signatures.

11. Determine how student work will be shared and assessed. Include this information with the contract. If rubrics or scoring guides are to be used, include them as well.

A graphic of these steps can be found on Blackline Master 45 (p. 151).

WebQuests

A WebQuest is an inquiry-based activity in which much of the material and information that students use is Internet based. WebQuests are effective because of their common structure and because they have teacher-chosen, embedded Web links within each project. Bernie Dodge of the University of San Diego is commonly thought of as the WebQuest guru. His WebQuest Page (http://www.webquest.org) has thousands of hits per day. It contains basic information on WebQuests, but perhaps the most useful feature is the matrix that shows subject/grade-level matches. Teachers could easily find several choices for existing WebQuests within a single topic. There are similar matrices on pages such as http://bestweb quests.com.

WebQuests can be used to differentiate in a number of ways. The WebQuests themselves are inquiry based, and many of them are based on some type of real-world scenario in which students are asked to assume a role within a task. Students can choose these roles based on their preferences. WebQuests are also a great way to have individual students or groups of learners extend their understanding of a topic by doing some independent work. They work particularly well for this purpose because they are very structured. You must ensure that the WebQuests will help students to meet or extend the required learning outcomes. Sites such as http://www.webquest.org and http://bestwebquests.com have a rating system so that teachers can choose WebQuests that have been reviewed and found to be of high quality. No matter where the WebQuest is located, it is important for teachers to ensure that links are accurate and functional.

Where to Start with WebQuests

- ◆ http://bestwebquests.com—This is a site that has a WebQuest matrix by grade and subject and rates each WebQuest with a star system, so you can quickly find those of high quality.

- ◆ http://webquest.org—This is Bernie Dodge's extensive site from the University of San Diego.

- ◆ For basic information, try a WebQuest on WebQuests:

  - • http://webquest.sdsu.edu/webquestwebquest-es.html (elementary version) or

  - • http://webquest.sdsu.edu/webquestwebquest-hum.html (middle/high school version).

  There is a great deal background material that would be suitable for a teacher workshop on WebQuests.

- ◆ http://www.ozline.com—This site contains information and links to WebQuests.

- http://www.techtrekers.com/webquests—Sorted by subject, this site also has short annotations for each WebQuest.

- http://www.kn.pacbell.com/wired/fil—This site contains a tool called "Filamentality" that enables you to create your own WebQuest without requiring any experience creating Web pages.

Creating a WebQuest

Before creating an original WebQuest, check to see whether a similar WebQuest already exists. If there isn't an exact match to your standards, it is certainly possible to take an existing WebQuest and adapt the activities for your particular group of students. If nothing is suitable, a WebQuest can be created. The components are as follows:

- Introduction: This first section introduces the focus of the project or topic, which often provides a real-life scenario.

- Task: This section outlines the general idea of the task in which students will engage. It should outline the learning outcomes that students will achieve by the completion of the project.

- Process: Step-by-step instructions are described so that students are able to complete the task independently. Handouts, checklists, or guiding questions may be provided.

- Evaluation: Evaluation tools and processes are made clear to the students. They should have these criteria prior to beginning the task.

- Conclusion: These activities help students bring some closure to the activity and often suggest ways in which their findings can be shared.

Steps to Create a WebQuest

1. Use curriculum documents to determine what you want the students to know, understand, and be able to do (KUDos).

2. Brainstorm a variety of tasks based on what you know about the learning preferences of your students.

3. Eliminate tasks that will not lead the students to KUDos.

4. Search for web sites that are of an appropriate reading level and contain information that students will need.

5. Design on an introduction or "hook" that will engage students in the task.

6. Describe the task(s) that the students will complete during the WebQuest.

7. Write step-by-step instructions for the WebQuest process and add the links students will use to find information.

8. Determine how student work will be assessed.

9. Decide how student work will be shared.

A graphic of these steps can be found on Blackline Master 46 (p. 152).

Using an Existing WebQuest

The tasks in a WebQuest can be used as written or adapted depending on your learning goals and the grade level of the learners. The benefit of having the links embedded means that students can focus on the task at hand rather than spending precious computer time doing ineffective or time-consuming searches. An added benefit is that WebQuests often include rubrics and checklists that correspond to the learning outcomes.

Technology Connection

If you are trying a WebQuest with young learners or students who have difficulty reading, try using a text-to-speech tool to help them understand the content of the linked pages. Macintosh Operating System X has a built-in text-to-speech tool, and others are free or very inexpensive to download (e.g., Universal Reader, http://www.premier-programming.com/UR/Ureader. htm, or Natural Reader, http://naturalreaders.com, both for Windows).

Tying Things Together

This chapter describes some of the activity structures that can support teachers in differentiating by learning preference. Using activity structures that provide learning preference choices can increase student engagement, but they must be designed with the specific learning outcomes in mind.

For Further Reflection

♦ How are the activity structures described in this chapter similar to and different from my current practices?

♦ How can I use or adapt these ideas to support differentiation by learning profile?

♦ How can I collaborate with colleagues to create lessons that are differentiated by learning profile?

4

Lessons Differentiated by Learning Preference

Benevolence alone will not make a teacher, nor will learning alone do it. The gift of teaching is a peculiar talent, and implies a need and a craving in the teacher himself.

John Jay Chapman

Studying lesson examples is an important step in learning about differentiated instruction. Having a picture of what instruction might look like helps teachers begin to think about differentiating with their own group of learners. This chapter contains a variety of lessons in several subject areas that are differentiated by learning preferences. There are examples of different models of intelligences, as well as examples of various activity structures.

Experimenting with lesson planning and implementation can be an important step on the road to differentiating instruction. Brendtro, Brokenleg, and Van Bockern, in their book *Reclaiming Youth at Risk,* describe this action orientation to teaching as "practice into theory." They hypothesize that beginning with experience is an effective way to develop successful practice. Busy teachers need examples of what is possible, and once they see the positive responses of students, they will be encouraged to learn more.

As you examine these lessons, keep in mind that they may not meet your exact curriculum standards or the needs of your particular group of students. Think about how these lessons could be used as a springboard to differentiate in an effective, meaningful way. Chapter 5 will provide some ideas about how you can adapt lessons and create original lessons of your own.

Language Arts

Book Report: Story Events Cube (Multiple Intelligences)

Learning goals: Students will—

Know: How to relate the important events of a story of choice.

Understand: Books have important events that tell a story.

Do: Describe the main events of a chosen book.

Figure 4.1. Story Events Cube

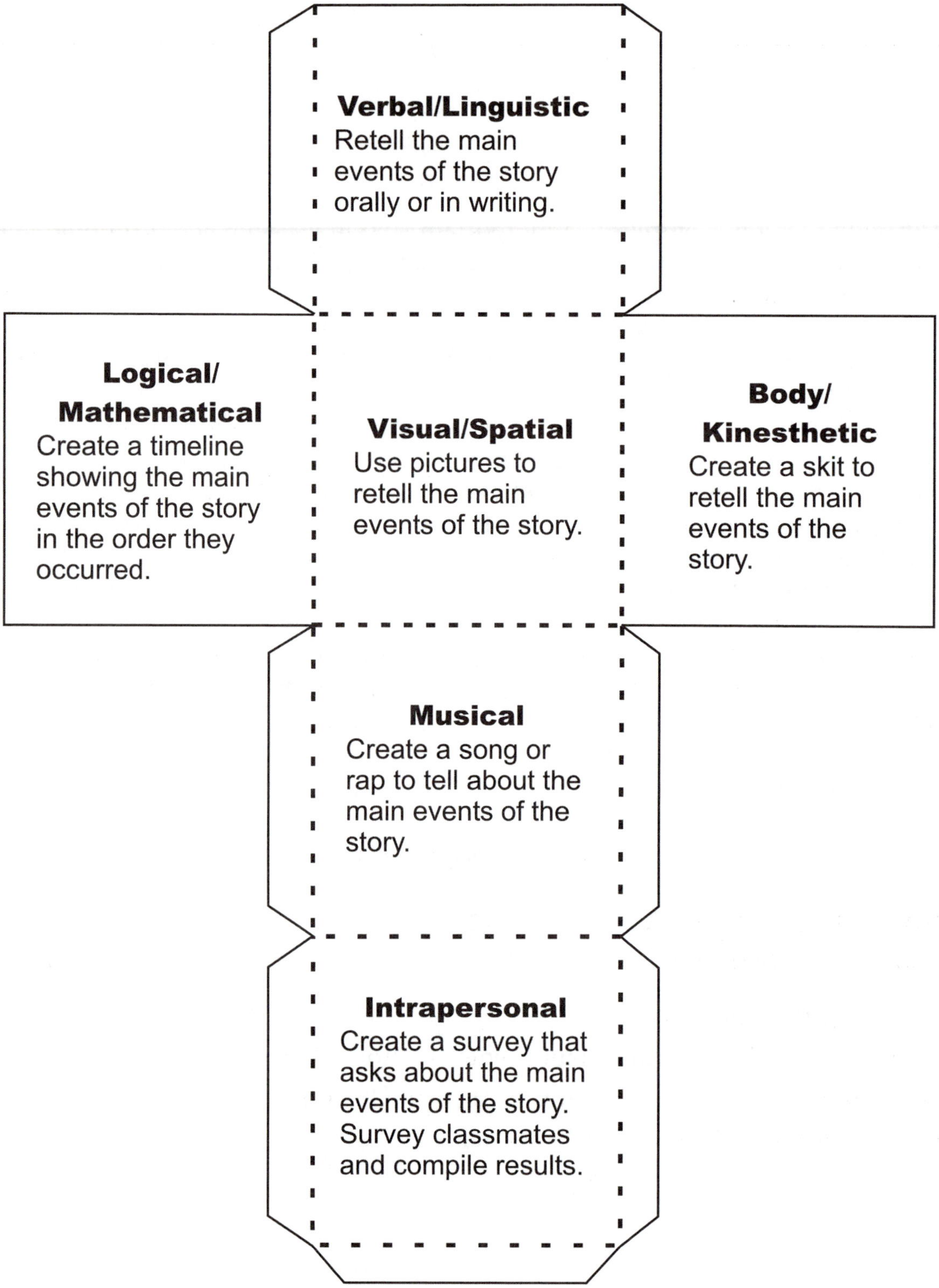

Verbal/Linguistic
Retell the main events of the story orally or in writing.

Logical/ Mathematical
Create a timeline showing the main events of the story in the order they occurred.

Visual/Spatial
Use pictures to retell the main events of the story.

Body/ Kinesthetic
Create a skit to retell the main events of the story.

Musical
Create a song or rap to tell about the main events of the story.

Intrapersonal
Create a survey that asks about the main events of the story. Survey classmates and compile results.

Story Response Choice Board (Triarchic)

Learning goals: Students will—

Know: The theme or message is the main idea that the writer wants to communicate.

Understand: Stories can be used to communicate a theme or message.

Do: Choose one of three ways to respond to a story that relates to the theme or message of the story that was read.

Analytical	Listen to or read a story and create a chart that lists events in the story and how they contribute to the theme of the story.
Practical	Think of a time you or someone you know was in a situation similar to the main character in the story. Draw and/or write about it and include the theme or message that was similar to the story.
Creative	Imagine that the story continues after the last page. Write or act out the next scene. This scene should relate to the theme or message of the story.

Fairy Tales: Learning Contract (Multiple Intelligences)

Learning goals: By completing the activities in this learning contract, students will—

Know:

The structure of fairy tales

The characteristics of fairy tales

Similarities and differences between different fairy tale versions

Understand:

Fairy tales have similar structures and characteristics.

Fairy tales are used to communicate a message.

Do: Compare and contrast different versions of the same fairy tale.

Students can choose from the following activities:

- *Activity 1 (Verbal/Linguistic):* Choose two or three versions of the same fairy tale. Use a Venn diagram to describe which elements of the story message are similar and which are different.

- *Activity 2 (Logical/Mathematical):* Create a chart that compares the similarities and messages of two or three versions of the same fairy tale.

- *Activity 3 (Musical/Rhythmic):* Create a song or rap that describes the similarities and differences between the messages between two versions of the same fairy tale.

- *Activity 4 (Body/Kinesthetic):* Dramatize two versions of a fairy tale in a way that shows the message and the similarities between the two stories.

- *Activity 5 (Visual/Spatial):* Create a poster or mural that demonstrates the message and the similarities between two or three versions of the same fairy tale.

- *Activity 6 (Interpersonal):* Create a game that demonstrates the message and the similarities between two or three versions of the same fairy tale.

- *Activity 7 (Intrapersonal):* Create a blog or journal from the point of view of one of the characters in a fairy tale. Compare the similarities and message between two versions of the fairy tale.

Activity chosen: _____

My activity will be complete and handed and/or ready to present by _____

Student signature: _____

Teacher signature: _____

Parent signature: _____

Spelling: Tic-Tac-Toe Board (Multiple Intelligences)

Learning goals: Students will—

Know: Spelling patterns.

Understand: Spelling patterns can be used to spell unfamiliar words.

Do: Generalize patterns by applying them to the correct spelling of new words

As a class: Review the spelling pattern. Brainstorm and classify words given by students.

Individually: Students choose three tasks to create a tic-tac-toe.

Verbal/Linguistic	*Logical/Mathematical*	*Visual/Spatial*
Write a commercial advertising your spelling pattern. Convince others of its importance by giving many examples of how the pattern is used in words.	Create as many groups for your spelling words, based on patterns or relationships you can find in the words.	Create a web or mind map with the spelling pattern in the middle.
Intrapersonal	*Free Choice*	*Naturalist*
Create a log book and record the words you find that fit the pattern and where you found them.	Think of way to demonstrate or remember words with the spelling pattern. Check your idea with your teacher first.	List as many words as you can find that relate to nature or the environment that fit the spelling pattern.
Body/Kinesthetic	*Musical*	*Intrapersonal*
Use a large piece of paper to write the letters in the spelling pattern in large letters. Use other pieces to make letters so new words can be formed by rearranging the letters. See how many words you can make in one minute. Challenge your friends.	Create a song or rap about the pattern and some of the words that can be created using the pattern.	With a partner, create a game to remember and practice the spelling pattern. Write instructions so other classmates can play it.

Parts of Speech RAFT

Learning goals: Students will—

Know: The meanings of key terminology to describe parts of speech (e.g., nouns, verbs, adverbs, and so on).

Understand: The parts of speech and how to use them to improve language.

Do: Create a product that demonstrates an understanding of different parts of speech, why they are important, and examples of how to use them.

Role	Audience	Format	Topic
Noun	Jury	Mock trial argument	Reasons why I think I'm the most important part of speech of all.
Verb	Other parts of speech	Invitation	I'm where all the action is!
Adjective	Dear Abby	Letter to an advice column (and response).	I'm tired of always helping out my friend, the noun.
Adverb	Other parts of speech	Lament	Why doesn't anyone ever remember what I do?
Pronoun	Other parts of speech	Cartoon strip	I feel like all I ever do is disguise myself as someone else.
Conjunction	Students	Song or rap	I bring things together.
Preposition	Students	Skit	I make relationships between parts of speech happen!

As a culmination of the activity, hold a "Parts of Speech Fair" with half of the students presenting their projects simultaneously in different parts of the room and the other half as the fair-goers. The fair-goers visit each student, who explains or performs his or her project, and they use the handout on the next page, "Parts of Speech Fair," to summarize what they learned. Switch roles and repeat so that all students have an understanding of each part of speech.

Parts of Speech Fair

Part of Speech	What It Is	Why It's Important	An Example

Math

Basic Facts Choice Board
(Visual Auditory Kinesthetic)

Learning goals: Students will—

Know: Basic facts of math.

Understand: Recall of basic facts can help with estimation, mental math, and speed of computation.

Do: Work on one of the choice board tasks to learn a set of math facts.

Coordinate Geometry Contract
(Visual Auditory Kinesthetic)

Learning goals: As a result of completing this learning contract, students will—

Know: How to describe, name, and interpret positions on a coordinate grid.

Understand: Coordinates can be used to find and name locations on a grid.

Do: Choose and complete tasks that demonstrate an understanding of how to specify locations using coordinate geometry

Hook: Play a class game or small group games of "Battleship."

Students should choose one core activity and one enrichment activity.

Core Activities

- *Core Activity 1 (Visual/Auditory):* Imagine that you are going to teach a younger group of students about coordinate geometry. Write, draw, or tell how you would help them to identify coordinate pairs. Use examples.

- *Core Activity 2 (Visual):* Create a mini book, chart, or cartoon with examples and pictures that illustrates key vocabulary:

  - Coordinate plane

  - Vertical axis

  - Horizontal axis

  - X-axis

  - Y-axis

  - Coordinate pairs

- *Core Activity 3 (Kinesthetic):* Tape a grid on the floor or a large sheet of plastic. Create coordinate pairs on cards and work with a partner to step to the coordinate pair on the grid. Check each other's work.

Enrichment Activities

- *Enrichment Activity 1:* Create a game using coordinate pairs. Use any materials you like.

- *Enrichment Activity 2:* Create a picture using straight lines on a coordinate grid. Identify the points on the picture so that a friend would be able to recreate the picture using the coordinates.

- *Enrichment Activity 3:* Research and find a job or task that would require the use of coordinate geometry. Explain the job or task and give an example of how coordinate geometry is used.

- *Enrichment Activity 4:* Create a rhyme, rap, or poem that explains how to find coordinate pairs on a coordinate plane.

- *Enrichment Activity 5:* Create a maze on a grid. Use coordinate pairs to provide an answer key that explains how to get from the starting point on the maze to the end of the maze.

Activities chosen:

Core activity: _____

Enrichment activity: _____

My activities will be complete and handed in by: _____

Student signature: _____

Teacher signature: _____

Parent signature: _____

Problem Solving: Cubing (Multiple Intelligences)

Learning goals: Students will—

Know: Steps to solve mathematical problems.

Understand: There are many different ways in which a problem might be solved.

Do: Explore different ways to find solutions to problems or situations.

Hook: Read a story about problem solving, such as "Grapes of Math" or "Math Potatoes: Mind-Stretching Brain Food" by Greg Tang.

The process is as follows:

- Discuss and model different ways to solve mathematical problems and the methods described on the task cube.

- Have students work in partners to solve a problem. They will use the cube to determine which method they will try.

- If the problem-solving method they have rolled will not be helpful in finding a solution, they should roll the cube again.

Figure 4.2. Task Cube

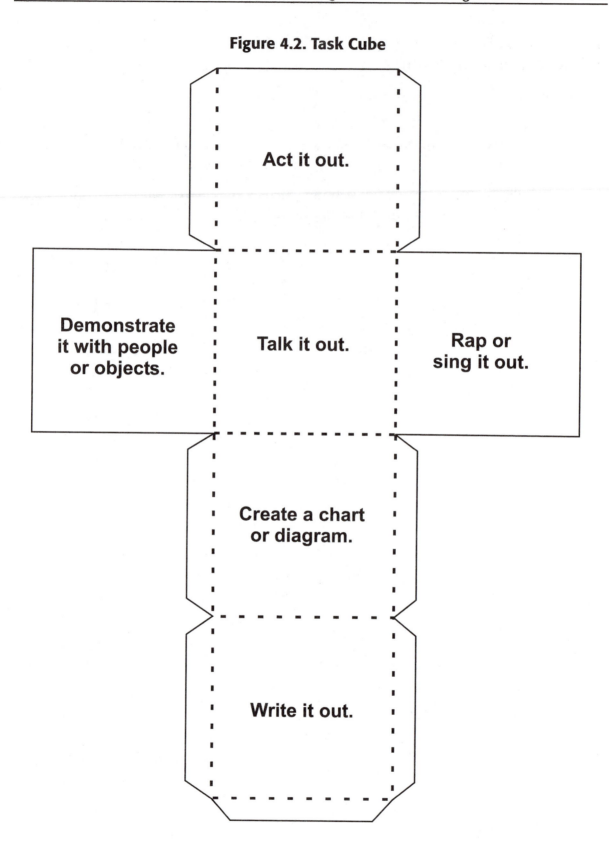

Symmetry RAFT
(Visual Auditory Kinesthetic)

Learning goals: Students will—

Know:

A line of symmetry divides a symmetrical figure, object or arrangement of objects into two parts that are congruent if one part is reflected or flipped over the line of symmetry.

Symmetry is when one half of a figure looks like the mirror image of the other half.

Asymmetry means "no symmetry" or "without symmetry."

Understand: Understanding symmetry, asymmetry, and line of symmetry can help to identify and create geometric figures.

Do: Create a product that demonstrates an understanding of symmetry, asymmetry, or line of symmetry.

Hook: Read a book about symmetry, such as *Let's Fly a Kite* by Stuart Murphy or *M Is for Mirror* by Duncan Birmingham.

Role	Audience	Format	Topic
Circle, square or other symmetrical shape	Students	Skit or demonstration (Kinesthetic)	Look at me, I've got symmetry!
A shape of your own creation that is not symmetrical	Self	Journal, song, poem or rap (Auditory)	Why I feel unbalanced
Line of symmetry	Shapes	Illustrated chart (Visual)	I make things even

For closure, have students share in groups so that there are one or more demonstrations of symmetry, asymmetry, and line of symmetry.

Science

Solar System: Cubing
(Visual Auditory Kinesthetic)

Learning goals: Students will—

Know: Our solar system includes the sun and planets.

Understand: Objects in the solar system have predictable characteristics and motion.

Do: Demonstrate an understanding of the parts of our solar system and their path around the sun.

Figure 4.3. Solar System Cube

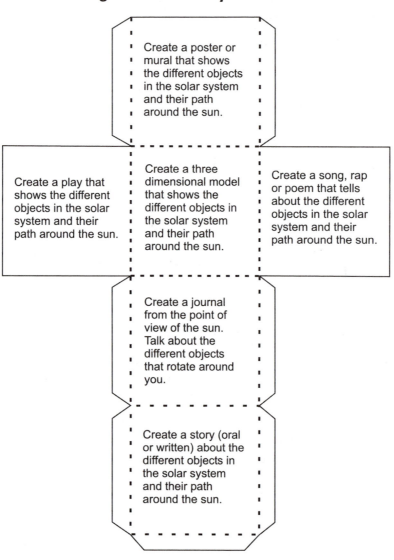

Plant and Animal Adaptations: RAFT
(Visual Auditory Kinesthetic)

Learning goals: Students will—

Know: Plants and animals have adaptations.

Understand: Plants and animals have structures or behaviors that help them survive in their environment.

Do: Create a product that will teach younger students about plant or animal adaptations that help them survive in their environment.

Role	Chosen plant or animal
Audience	Younger students
Format	Skit, children's book, cartoon, chart, song, rap or student (negotiated with the teacher) choice
Topic	"I will survive!" Teach younger students about how plants and animals have structures or behaviors that help them survive in their environment.

For closure, visit a class of younger students so that the projects can be shared. Discuss whether the students feel their projects were successful in helping the younger students understand adaptations.

Learning Contract
(Triarchic)

Learning goals: As a result of completing this learning contract, students will—

Know: The names and contributions of those who have made scientific innovations.

Understand: Diverse people have made important contributions to scientific innovations.

Do: Research a scientist who has made an important contribution to scientific innovation.

Hook: Watch a short video clip on a scientific innovation. Brainstorm the names of innovations or scientists that students would like to learn about.

Students can choose one of the following activities:

- *Activity 1 (Analytical):* Create a fact file for your chosen scientist. Explain his or her important contribution to scientific innovation.

- *Activity 2 (Practical):* Create a demonstration that shows about a scientific innovation used in real life. Tell about the scientist and why this innovation is important.

- *Activity 3 (Creative):* Create a commercial or story that tells about a scientific innovation. Tell about the scientist who created it and why this innovation is important.

Activity chosen:

My activity will be complete and handed in by: _____

Student signature: _____

Teacher signature: _____

Parent signature: _____

Rock Cycle: Choice Board
(Visual Auditory Kinesthetic)

Learning goals: Students will—

Know: The rock cycle can be used to describe the transition of rocks through geological time.

Understand: Rocks are constantly made, changed, destroyed, and made again.

Do: Demonstrate an understanding of the rock cycle through a chosen project.

Visual	Create a poster and use pictures and words (oral or written) to describe the rock cycle.
Auditory	Create a song, poem, or story to describe the rock cycle.
Kinesthetic	Use real objects to create a demonstration of the rock cycle.

Social Studies

Understanding Symbols: RAFT
(Visual Auditory Kinesthetic)

Learning goals: Students will—

Know: There are symbols associated with countries or regions.

Understand: Symbols are influenced by people and events from the past.

Do: Create a product that demonstrates an understanding of a symbol.

Hook: Read a story or look at photos or Web pages that show symbols of the country or region and brainstorm a list of important symbols.

Role	Symbol Chosen
Audience	Other citizens of the country or region
Format	Chart, poem, song, play, pictures (or other product—check your choice with your teacher first)
Topic	What events or people made me an important symbol of my country or region and why I am so important!

Choice Board (Triarchic)

Learning goals: Students will—

Know: The reasons for rules and laws and the consequences for people who violate rules and laws.

Understand: Laws protect individual rights and promote the common good.

Do: Create a product that demonstrates an understanding of rules, laws, and consequences.

Hook: Read a story that takes a humorous look at laws, such as one from *Chickens May Not Cross the Road and Other Crazy but True Laws* by Kathi Linz. Discuss classroom rules and why they are important, and then discuss community laws and consequences.

Figure 4.4. Choice Board

Analytical

Use a graphic organizer to list rules or laws in your school or community and what the consequences might be if they were broken.

Practical

Create a scenario, radio show or TV show that demonstrates what your city or town would be like if there were no laws and then a second where there were laws and consequences.

Creative

Create a fable and write or act it out. In the fable, describe what would happen if there were no laws in a certain situation. Include a moral to the story.

Settlers Learning Contract (Triarchic)

Learning goals: Students will—

Know: Who were the settlers in the region and what were some of the influences they had on the region over time.

Understand: Settlement influences the character of a region.

Do: Research the settlers who settled in their region and show how they have influenced the area over time.

Students should choose one core activity and one enrichment activity.

Core Activities

For the core activity chosen, be sure that your project demonstrates answers to these questions:

- Where did settlers in the region come from?

- What did they bring with them that have influenced the region over time? (e.g., traditions, values, culture, food, celebrations, etc.)

♦ *Core Activity 1 (Analytical):* Create a Venn diagram or chart that compares people in the region today and settlers from long ago. Compare and contrast the two groups to show similarities and differences and how settlers have influenced the region over time.

♦ *Core Activity 2 (Practical):* Convince someone you know to come and visit your region. Use the characteristics of your region that have been influenced by settlers as the reasons why it would be interesting to come. You can convince them through a monologue, letter, invitation (or other product you choose—check your proposal with your teacher).

♦ *Core Activity 3 (Creative):* Imagine you are a settler from long ago who has been dropped into the region today. Create a monologue, journal, or letter (or other product you choose—check your proposal with your teacher) that describes what you see and where you can still see influences from your time.

Enrichment Activities

- *Enrichment Activity 1:* Create a song or a poem that describes influences of settlers on your region.

- *Enrichment Activity 2:* Create a play or picture book for younger students that could help them understand the settlers' influences on your region.

- *Enrichment Activity 3:* Create a bumper sticker including a slogan that reflects a characteristic of your region that was influenced by settlers.

- *Enrichment Activity 4:* Take digital pictures or use other found photographs and use them to tell about settlers' influences on your region.

- *Enrichment Activity 5:* Create "Who am I?/What am I" riddles to identify regional characteristics that have been influence by settlers (e.g., landmarks, traditions, foods, culture, etc.).

Activities chosen:

Core activity: _____

Enrichment activity: _____

My activities will be complete and handed in by: _____

Student signature: _____

Teacher signature: _____

Parent signature: _____

Ancient Civilizations: Cubing
(Multiple Intelligences)

Learning goals: Students will—

Know: The geographic, political, economic, religious, cultural, and social structures of an ancient civilization.

Understand: Our understanding of why civilizations dominate or decline can be expanded by studying the people and events of ancient civilization.

Do: Create a product that demonstrates an understanding of aspects of ancient civilization.

The process is as follows:

- ◆ Roll the topic cube to determine the topic that will be explored.

- ◆ Roll the product cube to determine how understanding of the topic will be represented.

Figure 4.5. Ancient Civilizations Cube

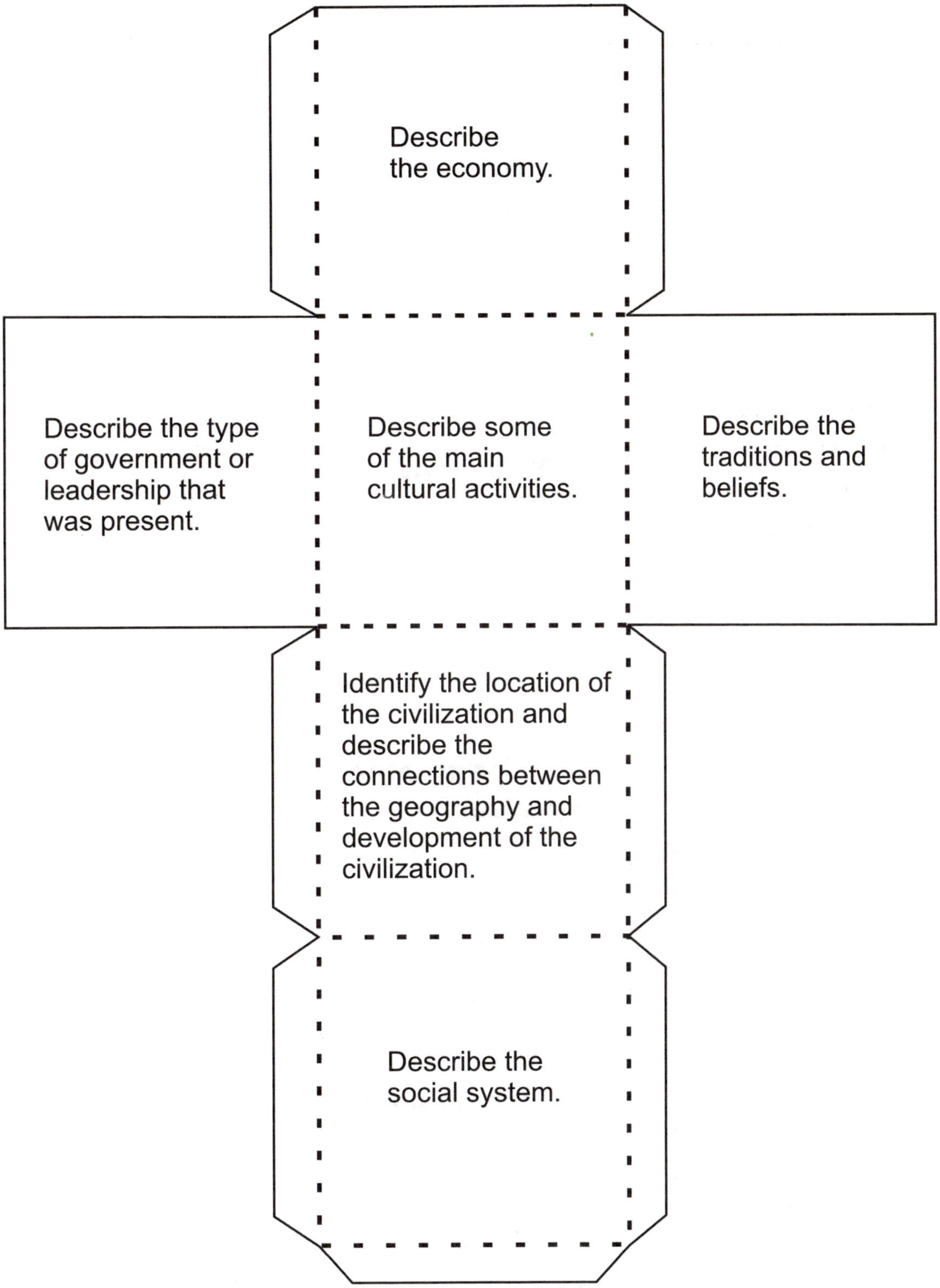

Describe
the economy.

Describe the type
of government or
leadership that
was present.

Describe some
of the main
cultural activities.

Describe the
traditions and
beliefs.

Identify the location of
the civilization and
describe the
connections between
the geography and
development of the
civilization.

Describe the
social system.

Figure 4.5. Product Cube

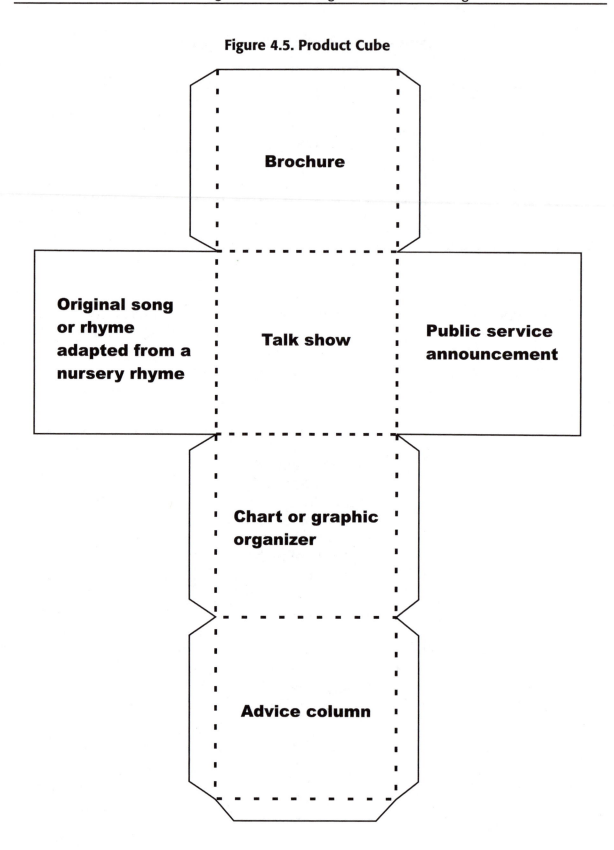

Tying Things Together

This chapter has provided a variety of sample lessons in different subject areas that are differentiated by learning preference. These lessons should be adapted to the unique needs your students or used as a resource to create new lessons. Chapter 5 will provide ideas about how these adaptations can be made and how new lessons can be created.

For Further Reflection

♦ In what way can these lessons help to support student learning profiles and increase engagement?

♦ How might I need to adapt these lessons to suit the needs of my learners and curriculum?

♦ What personal learning experiences have I had when I have been able to work in a preferred way, or had to work in a way that did not come easily? How did they feel?

5

Creating and Adapting Lessons

It is the supreme art of the teacher to awaken joy in creative expression and knowledge.

Albert Einstein

The real art in differentiating instruction is when a teacher is able to accurately assess students as learners and then create or adjust lessons accordingly. The lessons presented in the previous chapter may or may not fit your learners, but this chapter will outline how you can create new lessons or adapt existing ones.

Is It Worth It?

When teachers first begin to plan for differentiation, there's no doubt that it takes some extra time up front. Once the learning activities are organized, however, there is more time to do individual conferencing and small group teaching. The one thing you probably do not want to do is to spend a great deal of time planning to differentiate a lesson that isn't an important understanding in a unit of study. Be sure that you are planning for an outcome that is one of the key concepts that students must understand in a deep way. If the concept to be learned isn't as essential as the time it will take for students to complete (or for you to plan), it's probably better to choose another way to help students work through the concept. For example, if a video and short discussion will be enough for the students to get the idea, do that instead of a lengthier project.

Lesson Plan Template

Using a template may be helpful when organizing a new lesson that is differentiated by learning preference (Figure 5.1). A blank lesson plan template can be found on Blackline Master 48 (p. 154).

Steps to Create a Lesson
Differentiated by Learning Preference

The following steps may be used when creating a lesson that is differentiated by learning preference. A reproducible copy of these steps can be found on Blackline Master 47 (p. 153).

1. Identify the subject and topic of study.

2. Use curriculum documents to determine what you want the students to know, understand, and be able to do (KUDos).

3. Decide on an activity structure that will allow students to choose a task that interests them (e.g., choice board, RAFT, cubing activity, learning contract, WebQuest, etc.).

4. Brainstorm a variety of tasks based on what you know about the learning preferences of your students.

5. Eliminate tasks that will not lead the students to KUDos.

6. Choose the activities that will be the most engaging for your students and best match their learning preferences.

7. Check to see that all students will reach the same KUDos, no matter which task(s) they complete.

8. Describe the learning activities in detail. Create student handouts, if appropriate.

9. Determine how student work will be assessed.

10. Decide how you will facilitate sharing and bring closure to the lesson.

Figure 5.1. Differentiating by Learning Preferences: Lesson Plan Template

Subject: **Topic:**

Outcomes: As a result of this study, students should:
   Know:
 	
   Understand:
 	
   Be able to do:

Learning Preference Model
 	
   ❑ Visual Auditory Kinesthetic
   ❑ Multiple Intelligences
   ❑ Triarchic
   ❑ Other

Activity Structure:
 	
   ❑ Choice Board   ❑ RAFT
   ❑ Cube   ❑ Learning Contract
   ❑ WebQuest   ❑ Other

Description of Learning Activities:
Assessment:
Closure/Sharing:

Adapting Lessons

The benefit of a book such as this one is that viewing lesson examples can provide a sense of what differentiation might look like in the classroom. After that, you can take the ideas and then adapt them to their specific student needs.

At the forefront of planning is *who* your students are and *where* they are in terms of readiness, interest, and learning preferences. Once this is established, you can critically look at lessons and decide whether they can be used as is or whether they need to be adapted. You may need to adapt them in some of the following ways:

- The text may need to be enlarged or simplified for younger learners or made more explicit for older or more advanced learners
- The number of task choices may need to be increased or reduced.
- The complexity of the tasks may need to be increased or reduced.
- The time required to complete the task may need to be adjusted.
- The evaluation criteria may need to be adjusted.
- The process of the tasks, including grouping or working individually, may need to be adjusted.

Additional choices may need to be added or removed to reflect the learning preferences of each group of learners.

It is also helpful to study lesson examples as a collaborative school team. The more examples teachers have to look through, the more ideas they are able to generate themselves.

Project Choice Ideas

Whether creating lessons from scratch or adapting an existing one, it may be helpful to scan through a list of projects that can be used for learning preference choices (Figure 5.2). Blackline Masters 49–51 (p. 155-158) contain project ideas for visual auditory kinesthetic, multiple intelligences, and triarchic lessons.

Figure 5.2. Triarchic Intelligences Project Ideas

Analytical	Practical	Creative
chart	scenario	picture
graphic organizer	role play	doodle
timeline	WebQuest	song
Venn diagram	job shadowing	invention
t-chart	dialog	riddles
patterns	newscast	commercial
sequencing	letter to the editor	mime
classifying	flyer	sculpture
definitions	scenario	play
cause/effect	role play	drama
code	demonstration	speech
graph	experiment	mural
database	real-world problem	fairy tale
blueprints	survey	monologue
newspaper	field trip	bumper sticker
fact file	petition	travelogue

Tying Things Together

This chapter has provided ideas that can help in creating and adapting lessons that are differentiated by learning preference. Keep in mind that they are only idea starters—they may not fit your standards or the needs of your particular learners. They will be helpful, however, as you begin to think about planning lessons for diverse groups of students. Chapter 6 will discuss other issues, including grouping in a differentiated classroom.

For Further Reflection

♦ How will I determine when I am able to use existing lessons and when I will need to adapt them?

♦ With whom might I be able to collaborate to create new lessons?

♦ How will I ensure that lessons used and created meet the needs of my learners as well as the important understandings that come from required curriculum and standards?

6

Managing a Differentiated Classroom

That students differ may be inconvenient, but it is inescapable.
Adapting to that diversity is the inevitable price of productivity.

Theodore Sizer

There are many issues and questions that teachers may have as they begin to differentiate in their classrooms. These may include thinking about how to begin creating a classroom climate to support differentiation, teaching routines that will facilitate group work, and different strategies for encouraging students to be active learners.

Creating a Positive Classroom Climate

Creating a sense of belonging is an important part of any successful classroom. It is particularly important in a differentiated classroom because there must be a foundation of trust and respect among all classroom members in order for it to be emotionally safe for students to do different kinds of work. Part of what makes differentiation possible is creating an environment where differences and unique talents are recognized and celebrated. Consider some of the following ideas that could be used to emphasize a positive classroom climate.

Surprising but True Stories

Share stories with students that tell about people who struggled early in life or in their career but went on to become successful. Some sources for these stories include books such as the *Chicken Soup for the Soul* series. A sample of such people can be found in Figure 6.1. Students could research and share stories about such people. A task card with a related assignment can be found on Blackline Master 52 (p. 158).

Figure 6.1. Surprising but True Stories

- Albert Einstein, scientist, was unable to speak fluently at age nine.
- Charles Shultz, creator of the *Peanuts* cartoon strip had his drawings for his high school rejected.
- Elvis Presley, famed musician, wasn't chosen for his high school singing club.
- Bill Gates of Microsoft failed with his first business idea, a device that could record information about traffic.
- Michael Jordan, basketball player, was cut from his high school basketball team.
- James McNeill Whistler, creator of the famous painting *Whistler's Mother*, failed out of military school because of poor grades in chemistry before he discovered his talent in art.
- Woody Allen, Academy Award–winning writer, producer, and director, failed motion picture production and English in college.
- Theodor Geisel, the writer better known as Dr. Seuss, was asked to step down as the editor in chief of his college newspaper.

Children's Literature

Picture books are incredibly powerful. They can be used to create an atmosphere of acceptance for all different kinds of learners and can be used at almost any grade level. The following is a list of literature that you could use as read-alouds to build a classroom climate that supports differentiated instruction. The kinds of follow-up activities that could be created after using these books as a springboard are endless. A complete list of these titles, suitable for reproducing and sharing with teachers, can be found on Blackline Master 53 (p. 159).

All the Colors of the Earth by Sheila Hamanaka

Amazing Grace by Mary Hoffman

Being Friends by Karen Beaumont

Chrysanthemum by Kevin Henkes

A Color of His Own by Leo Lionni

Crow Boy by Taro Yashima

Do You Want to Be My Friend? by Eric Carle

The Dot by Peter Reynolds

Frederick by Leo Lionni

Music

Music can be used to help create a caring and accepting classroom climate. You might consider creating a compilation of such songs that could be played when students enter the classroom or during any other transition time. You may also consider having a "class song" that is sung as a way to remind students of how they are important members of the group. Songs and collections that could be used to promote a positive climate could include the following:

- "The World is a Rainbow" by Greg Scelsa
- "You Are Special" by Fred Rogers
- "Beautiful Rainbow World" by Daria A. Marmaluk-Hajioannou
- "It's Not Easy Being Green" by Jim Henson
- "Peace in Our Land: Children Celebrating Diversity" by Bunny Hull
- "Circle of Peace" by Carol Johnson
- "Come Join the Circle: Songs for Peacemaking" by Paulette Meier
- "Peace It Together" by Mary Miche

Routines: The Ultimate Proactive Tool

Having a caring classroom climate is an important part of a differentiated classroom, but there are other components necessary to ensure that the classroom runs smoothly. Many difficulties can be avoided by establishing routines at the beginning of the year and then reinforcing them throughout the year. If students know how to do things such as entering the classroom, how to find resources, and how to hand in work, classroom life will be much smoother than if there are no established routines.

The following eight-step process works well in teaching classroom routines:

1. Create a large chart with numbered steps describing the routine.
2. Explain it verbally while going through the steps on the chart.
3. Model exactly how you would like the routine done.
4. Check for understanding.
5. Practice with students.
6. Post the chart on a wall in the classroom.
7. Reinforce the routine.
8. Reteach as often as necessary.

The Eight Steps in Detail

1. **Create a large chart with numbered steps, describing the routine.** This provides a visual cue to students so that as they are learning the routines, they understand exactly what to do. It also gives a reference point for any reteaching that needs to happen and helps students understand that the routines are part of classroom expectations every day.

2. **Explain it verbally while going through the steps on the chart.** Explaining the routine verbally while referring to the chart helps students who may be auditory learners to think about and understand exactly what the steps in the routine entail.

3. **Model exactly how you would like the routine done.** As if you were a student, model the routine while talking through the steps on the chart. This helps students get a picture of exactly what is expected as they engage in the routine.

4. **Check for understanding.** After modeling, allow time for students to ask any questions. It might also be helpful to have students turn to a partner and discuss what the routine is and why it is necessary.

5. **Practice with students.** Have students practice the routine two or three times so that they understand what it will look like in the classroom. This active practice will help to reinforce the routine with kinesthetic learners.

6. **Post the chart on a wall in the classroom.** Once the routine has been practiced, post the chart with the routine at the front of the classroom so that it can be revisited as needed. As it becomes habit and you teach a new routine, it may be placed in a less prominent spot and replaced with a chart for a new routine or one you wish to review.

7. **Reinforce the routine.** As students perform the routine the way you would like, reinforce this behaviour. This can be done with verbal praise or with other reinforcement.

8. **Reteach as often as necessary.** This might be one of the most often forgotten yet important steps. Teachers do a fine job of establishing rules and routines early in the year. The difficulty seems to start after students have been together for a while and they may not have the routines firmly in their minds—they may test to see whether they still apply. If you find that the routines are not working well, put the poster with the steps of the routine back up in a prominent place and go through Steps 1–5 again. Revisiting routines as soon as they seem to be less effective is an excellent way to maintain a sense of order in the classroom.

Avoid teaching several routines at the same time, as students might become confused. Start with the those that are most crucial to the effective running of the classroom and then add new ones as they are needed. The age and characteristics of the students in the classroom will determine what kinds of routines you will need to establish and reinforce.

Ideas to Create Opportunities for Active Learning

Another way to support student learning and help them stay on task is to have them actively involved in their learning. Incorporating active learning strategies helps to provide a variety of tasks and movement. The following is a list of cooperative learning activities that could be used. A compilation of these strategies can also be found on Blackline Master 54 (p. 161).

- **Card Sort:** The teacher (or students) prepare two sets of cards. One set should have terminology and the second set should contain corresponding definitions. Students work in teams to find matches. It can be helpful if the terms and definitions sets are done on two different colors of paper.

- **Carousel Brainstorming:** The teacher posts chart paper on the wall with key questions or ideas at the top. Groups are formed and one person scribes for the group and adds to the chart as they brainstorm. When prompted, groups move to a new chart, read other groups' responses, and add to the ideas. Teams may use a different color of felt pen so that it is easy to ask questions of groups if ideas are not clear.

- **Find the Expert:** The teacher polls the class to see which students have special knowledge to share on a topic. Those students become the experts and stand in different parts of the room. The remaining students are divided evenly into groups and sit around an expert. They listen as the student explains his or her special understanding of the topic and then ask questions of him or her. They could also take notes, if appropriate. Groups rotate around the room until they have had an opportunity to hear from each expert.

- **Four Corners:** The teacher poses a question and gives four potential responses and points to a corner for each one (or the teacher might want to post a visual cue in each corner in advance). Students move to their chosen corner and discuss the topic with those who also chose that corner. The students then come together for a whole-class discussion.

- **Gallery Walk with Docent:** After teams have generated ideas on a topic using a piece of chart paper, they appoint a "docent" to stay with their work. Teams rotate around, examining other team's ideas and asking questions of the docent. Teams then meet together to discuss and add to their information so that the docent also can learn from other teams.

- **Graffiti:** Groups receive a large piece of paper and felt pens of different colors. Students generate ideas and write them quickly as if they were creating graffiti on a wall. Groups can move to other papers carousel style and discuss or add to the ideas of other groups, if desired.

- **Human Continuum:** The teacher poses a question or problem and students line up according to their opinion on the answer. The teacher can then discuss the distribution of the group or prompt students to discuss their reasoning for choosing their spot on the continuum with one or two people nearby.

- **Inside/Outside Circles:** The teacher divides class in half. One group forms a circle and then turns to face outward. Those from the remaining group find one person in the circle to stand opposite (so there are two circles of people facing each other). Information can be shared and reviewed, and the outer circle can move easily (e.g., The teacher could call, "Outside circle people, move three places to the right.") to generate more responses or discuss new information.

- **Jigsaw:** "Home groups" using a small number of students (i.e., three to six students) are formed. Each home group member is assigned a number. Students then move to an "expert group" containing others who have the same number (e.g., All "number ones" together). They read a short section of information from a textbook (or other material) independently and then work together to decide what is important. After discussion in these "expert groups," everyone returns to their "home group" and each expert teaches his or her portion of the material. The teacher may want to provide a graphic organizer so that each student leaves the home group with a set of notes that covers all of the important points.

- **Lineups:** Students line up according to a prompt by the teacher. Examples might be to line up by house number, birthday month, etc. They then discuss with an elbow partner (someone with whom they can touch elbows without changing place in the line) or in a small group.

- **Most Stay, One Strays:** Students work in a team to solve a problem. While they work, they send one member out periodically to "stray" to other groups to bring new ideas back to the team.

- **Number Heads Problem Solving:** Students sit in groups and each group member is given a number. The teacher poses a problem, and all four students discuss so that each is able to respond to the question. The teacher calls a number and that student is responsible for sharing for the group.

- **Pass a Problem:** The teacher creates problems for teams to solve and writes them on or attaches them to envelopes. Teams read the problems, place their solutions in the envelope, and then exchange with another team to check their solution and discuss how they solved the problem and whether they believe the answer to be correct. The teacher debriefs by providing the solution and giving groups time to share the different ways that teams solved the problem.

♦ **Round-Robin Brainstorming:** The class is divided into small groups with one person appointed as the recorder. A question is posed, and students are given time to think about and write their answers individually. Next, members of the team share responses with one another, round-robin style. The recorder writes down the ideas of the group members.

♦ **Say and Switch:** Partners take turns responding to a topic given by the teacher at signalled times. The times will be unpredictable and the person listening must pick up from their partner's train of thought before adding new ideas.

♦ **Send a Question:** Students work in teams to write a review question or problem on a card and ask other teams to solve it. The team that writes the question determines whether the groups have come up with a solution.

♦ **Talking Chips:** Students are given a certain number of chips. Each time they talk, they must submit a chip, but once their chips are gone they may no longer talk. Students are encouraged to use all their chips.

♦ **ThinkPad Brainstorming:** Students individually brainstorm and write down their answers on a pad of scrap paper. Once they are done, they share their information with a partner or a team.

♦ **Think/Pair/Share:** First, individuals think silently about a question posed by the teacher. Student pair up and exchange thoughts. Finally, the pairs share their responses with the whole class.

♦ **Think/Ink/Pair/Share:** This strategy uses same process as think/pair/share, except that after students have time to think, they are asked to "ink" or write their ideas on paper before they share.

♦ **Think/Pair/Square:** This is the same process as think/pair/share, except that partners share with another set of partners before the whole-class discussion.

♦ **Three-Minute Intermission:** The teacher stops any time during a class discussion, story, video, or other learning experience and gives partners or teams three minutes to review what has been said and to ask clarifying questions.

♦ **Three-Step Interview:** Partners interview each other about themselves or a subject-specific topic. They then find another team and form a group of four. Each person shares what they learned from the original partner.

♦ **Two Facts and a Fib:** Students or the teacher write down two facts and one idea that is not true. Each team tries to identify which is which. This can be done using personal experiences or subject-related material.

♦ **Visible Quiz:** The teacher poses questions with multiple-choice responses and students sit in teams and discuss the responses. When the teacher asks, they hold up their answers and may be called on to explain their team's reasoning.

From St. Albert Protestant Schools Alberta Initiative for School Improvement Project. Used with permission.

Tying Things Together

Managing the differentiated classroom essentially involves classroom management techniques that would be effective in any environment. It may, however, be even more important when differentiating because it is essential that students feel there is structure but opportunities for active learning. Once this atmosphere has been created, students feel that it is part of the normal course of business that students do different things at different times during the school day, but within an atmosphere of predictability and emotional safety.

For Further Reflection

♦ How do I create a positive environment in my classroom?

♦ How do I teach routines so that there is predictability and structure within my classroom?

♦ What techniques do I presently use to ensure students are actively engaged in learning? What new ideas could I incorporate?

♦ Where might I find additional resources and expertise in activities to create a positive classroom climate and ensure active engagement?

7

How to Begin

Hope is contagious. Its infection inspires. Let us come to each day with hope. Not because we should but because we can.

Noah benShea

Hope is an interesting thing. Without it, it is easy to become paralyzed, and this can happen to both students and teachers. For students, understanding that they have learning strengths gives them hope, and this is especially true for learners who may be feeling discouraged. Working within an area of strength gives students confidence that they can learn and eventually take risks. For teachers, providing practical ideas to differentiate instruction that can be implemented immediately gives them hope that differentiating instruction is possible. Because differentiated instruction is such a large field of study, this series of books endeavors to focus on one aspect of differentiating at a time. With this in mind, there are things that teachers can do to continue to move forward in the journey to differentiate instruction.

Assess Student Learning Preferences

Begin by discovering student learning preferences, especially with the students who don't tend to share this information readily. It is not enough just to find out; we must also be prepared to use this information to provide different kinds of learning experiences. Consider using online surveys if you are working with large numbers of students.

Have a System to Record Learning Preferences

Find some way to record student learning preferences so that they are stored in a system that is easy to use. This will help facilitate planning and help you be more responsive to the needs of each group of students. This could include the use of existing recordkeeping templates in a plan book, index cards, a computer database, or anything else that will help you find information easily. Blackline Masters 32–35 (pp. 138-141) provide recordkeeping tools that can be used to create such a system.

Reflect

Either informally or through the use of a teacher self-assessment, think about your own learning preferences. How do they influence the way you tend to teach in the classroom? An example of a teacher self-reflection tool can be found on Blackline Master 36. As you differentiate by student learning preference, reflect on the process. Are students able to learn more effectively? How do they feel about learning in preferred and nonpreferred modalities?

Track

Over a period of a week or two, jot down the learning preferences that are the focus of your teaching. Note any trends you see. Make plans to diversify the ways in which you present and help your students process information. If thinking about offering multiple activities to students in one lesson is overwhelming, consider focusing on using different learning preferences during large group instruction. Set goals for yourself, such as ensuring that all intelligences areas are the focus of instruction at least once per week in whole-group instruction. Use tools (Figure 7.1) such as the ones found on Blackline Masters 55–57 (pp. 163-165) to help you balance the different learning preferences over time.

Figure 7.1. Multiple Intelligences Tracking Tool

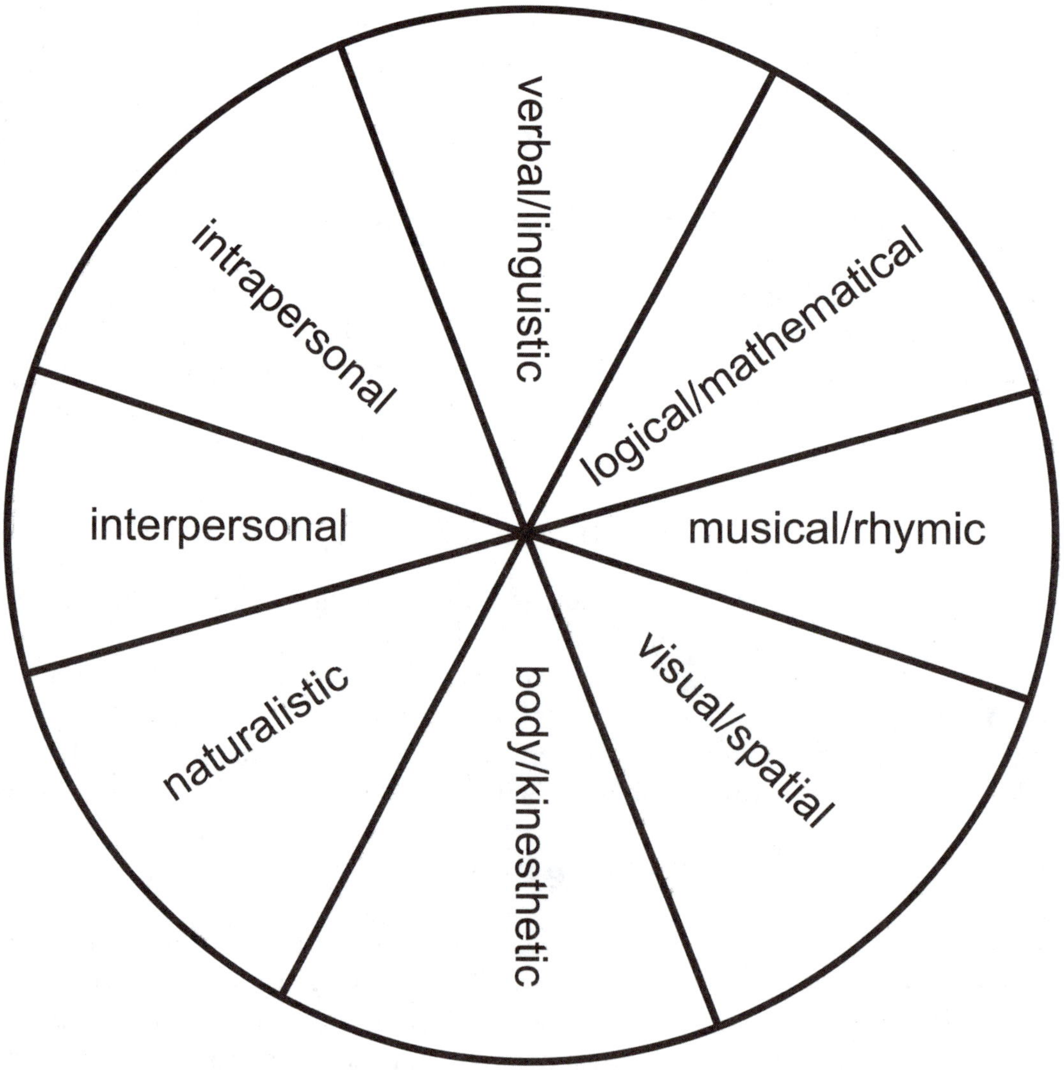

Don't Reinvent the Wheel

To begin with, it might be easier to use an existing differentiated lesson or adapt a traditional lesson that is already written than to start from scratch. With WebQuests, for example, there are hundreds of them out on the World Wide Web. Make sure these lessons fit your learning outcomes, and if they don't, adapt them. Once you have tried some lessons, it is much easier to create new ones, and eventually, it just becomes a part of how you think about planning.

Work Together

Creating lesson plans and strategies is much easier to do when working with colleagues. Consider meeting with a group of colleagues who teach a similar grade or subject and create a lesson plan portfolio. Share what has been created in a binder or consider high-tech collaboration tools such as blogs, wikis, or moodles.

Technology Connection

Shared folders on a school network can be used to store copies of lesson plans that all teachers can access. Wikis are another way to share products created electronically, and teachers can access them from any computer with an Internet connection. Teachers can add lesson plans to a common place and others can take the lesson plans, download, and use them. In addition, the lesson plans can be adapted and saved as new versions. There are many places to create wikis for free, such as http://wikispaces.com.

Consider Schoolwide Initiatives

Some schools have implemented learning preferences initiatives schoolwide, and even bill themselves as such (for example, some schools call themselves a "multiple intelligences school"). Having all staff members engage in professional development and work together toward implementing such initiatives can produce a kind of momentum that can be powerful. For example, some schools display posters on multiple intelligences in every classroom. A set of posters for each of the three models used in this book can be found from Blackline Masters 8–21 (pp. 114-127). These could be enlarged and mounted on construction paper for use in classrooms or common areas.

There are some interesting resources, such as *The Multiple Intelligences School: A Place for all Students to Succeed* by Sue Teele and Chapter 9, "The MI School," in Thomas Armstrong's *Multiple Intelligences in the Classroom*, that can provide a framework to do such planning, and examples of schools that have embarked on large-scale initiatives. Howard Gardner (1999, pp. 91–92) provides some interesting perspectives and caution about such initiatives. He writes,

> When visiting a so-called MI school, I look for signs of personalization: evidence that all involved in the educational encounters take differences among human beings seriously and that they construct curricula, pedagogy, and assessment in the light of these difference. Overt attention to MI theory and to my efforts means little if the children are treated in a homogenized way. By the same token, whether or not staff members have ever heard of MI theory, I would happily send my children to a school that takes differences among children seriously, that shared knowledge about differences with children and parents, that encourages children to assume responsibility for their own learning, and that presents materials in such a way that each child has the maximum opportunity to master those materials and to show others and themselves what they have learned and understood.

Start Small

It isn't possible to differentiate all the time, every day. Whole-class instruction is still important as you build common vocabulary and a sense of community. Start with one lesson that is an adaptation of what you already do and build on that success.

Enjoy the Journey

Remember that learning to differentiate isn't a destination but a journey, so celebrate your efforts along the way. This book has aimed to stretch your thinking about learning preferences and give you practical ideas about how you can continue with this important work. A poem that illustrates the importance of valuing and nurturing students, just as they are, is called, "Children Are Like Trees":

Children are very much like trees.
They differ in kind and form.
Some have grown in the open with lots of space to expand.
Others have been affected by the pressure of the forest around them.
Some have been tied to sticks to keep them straight, while
Others have been allowed to develop naturally, with a minimum of pruning.
Some children are made of hard wood; others of soft.

Like trees which may be best for shade, or fruit, or decoration
Children have their best uses.
Some are better to look at; some are better in groups;
Others are better standing alone.

Some grow strong and sturdy; others need protection from the elements
But every wood, every tree, and every child has a unique and different value. We
may try to graft the characteristics of a child onto another,
But we know we cannot make a palm tree into an oak or vice versa.

The best we can do is to accept the tree as it is, to feed it, to give it light, and to
prune it gently to its natural shape. And we need to remember that in working
with children, as well as in working with wood…

For best results, always sand with the grain.

—Anonymous

Blackline Masters

Blackline Master 1:
Student Learning Preferences Inventory

Name _____ **Date** _____

Circle the face that best describes how you feel about the following statements:

1. I like working with others.

2. I like to do jigsaw puzzles and mazes.

3. I like quiet places.

4. I like sports.

5. I like music.

6. I like playing alone.

7. I like activity and noise.

8. I like working with numbers.

9. I like being outside.

Name _____ **Date** _____

Circle the face that best describes how you feel about the following statements:

10. I like school.   ☺ 😐 ☹

11. I like poems and rhymes.   ☺ 😐 ☹

12. Other things I like:

13. Things I don't like:

14. Things I'd like to improve are:

15. Something else you should know about me is:

Blackline Master 2:
Student Learning Preferences Inventory

Name_____ Date_____

1. What are your hobbies? How much time do you spend on them?

2. What are your favorite activities at school and why?

3. How are you smart?

4. What is your favorite activity at school and why?

5. How do you like to learn about things? (e.g., reading, hands-on, watching demonstrations, talking to others, writing ideas out)

6. What do you think you might want to do as a career when you are an adult?

7. When you have free time at home, what do you like to do?

8. What is one thing you can do very well?

9. What else is important for people to know about you?

Blackline Master 3:
Visual Auditory Kinesthetic (VAK) Inventory

Teacher directions:

1. Distribute copies of the Visual Auditory Kinesthetic Graph to each student.

2. Explain to students that you will be reading about three different ways of learning and that you will use the information to find out more about how they like to learn. They are to listen to each set of descriptions and then decide on a scale of 1 to 10 how much the description sounds like themselves, where 1 means "This doesn't sound like me at all" and 10 means "This sounds exactly like me." Students will choose a number between 1 and 10 to help describe the degree to which each way of learning sounds like themselves.

3. Assure students that there is no wrong or right answer and that they are just giving an estimate.

4. Once they have estimated a number between 1 and 10, they will shade the bar graph to indicate the number they have chosen. Read one set of descriptors at a time and then pause to give students enough time to shade each column of the graph.

5. You may wish to model an example on an overhead as you go.

   Visual

   - You enjoy learning through reading and visuals.
   - You can easily visualize people, places and things.
   - You enjoy games like jigsaw puzzles and mazes.
   - You can read graphs and maps easily.
   - Rate yourself from 1 to 10.

   Auditory

   - You can remember what to do after hearing instructions.
   - You enjoy listening to music.
   - You enjoy listening to audiobooks or talk radio.
   - You talk out loud to yourself when trying to remember things.
   - Rate yourself from 1 to 10.

   Kinesthetic

   - You find yourself fidgeting often.
   - You use hand gestures or other kinds of body language to express yourself.
   - You prefer hands-on learning to reading something or hearing about it.
   - You enjoy physical activities such as sports or dancing.
   - Rate yourself from 1 to 10.

Visual Auditory Kinesthetic Graph

Name _____

Visual	**Auditory**	**Kinesthetic**

Blackline Master 4:
Multiple Intelligences Inventory

Teacher directions:

1. Distribute copies of the Multiple Intelligences Graph to each student.

2. Explain to students that you will be reading about eight different ways of learning and that you will use the information to find out more about how they like to learn. They are to listen to each set of descriptions and then decide on a scale of 1 to 10 how much the description sounds like themselves, where 1 means "This doesn't sound like me at all" and 10 means "This sounds exactly like me." Students will choose a number between 1 and 10 to help describe the degree to which each way of learning sounds like themselves.

3. Assure students that there is no wrong or right answer and that they are just giving an estimate.

4. Once they have estimated a number between 1 and 10, they will shade the bar graph to indicate the number they have chosen. Read one set of descriptors at a time and then pause to give students enough time to shade each column of the graph.

5. You may wish to model an example on an overhead as you go.

Verbal/Linguistic

- You can easily express yourself either orally or in writing.
- You enjoy reading.
- You enjoy word puzzles and games such as Scrabble.
- You like to talk through problems.
- Rate yourself from 1 to 10.

Logical/Mathematical

- You enjoy working with numbers, and math is one of your favorite subjects
- You enjoy logic or strategy games such as chess or checkers.
- You can easily spot patterns.
- You prefer a step-by-step approach to problem solving.
- Rate yourself from 1 to 10.

Visual/Spatial

- You can visualize things easily.
- You are good at directions and remembering how to locate places you've been.
- You enjoy doodling and drawing.
- You can visualize how things look from a different perspective.
- Rate yourself from 1 to 10.

Body/Kinesthetic

+ You enjoy different kinds of physical activities such as sports or dancing.
+ You tend to fidget if sitting for a long period of time.
+ You use your hands and body when you talk.
+ You prefer to handle things while learning about them, rather than having someone show you about it or tell you about it.
+ Rate yourself from 1 to 10.

Musical/Rhythmic

+ Usually, you can remember songs easily.
+ You often listen to music.
+ You find yourself tapping in time to music.
+ You can remember things if you put them to music or to a rhythm.
+ Rate yourself from 1 to 10.

Naturalist

+ You like pets and other animals.
+ You can recognize many different types of trees, flowers, and plants.
+ You feel most comfortable when surrounded by nature.
+ You feel strongly about environmental issues such as global warming.
+ Rate yourself from 1 to 10.

Interpersonal

+ You enjoy working in a group.
+ You enjoy getting involved in after school activities that involve socialization.
+ You would rather talk over problems with others rather than trying to solve them by yourself.
+ You are good at understanding how people feel and like to help others.
+ Rate yourself from 1 to 10.

Intrapersonal

+ You keep a personal diary or blog.
+ You are aware of your own feelings and can express them.
+ You are an independent thinker and are not easily influenced by other people.
+ You enjoy doing activities that you can do by yourself.
+ Rate yourself from 1 to 10.

Multiple Intelligences Graph

Name _____

Verbal/ Linguistic	Logical/ Mathematical	Musical/ Rhythmic	Visual/ Spatial	Body/ Kinesthetic	Naturalist	Interpersonal	Intrapersonal

Blackline Master 5:
Triarchic Intelligences Inventory

Teacher directions:

1. Distribute copies of the Triarchic Intelligences Graph to each student.

2. Explain to students that you will be reading about three different ways of learning and that you will use the information to find out more about how they like to learn. They are to listen to each set of descriptions and then decide on a scale of 1 to 10 how much the description sounds like themselves, where 1 means "This doesn't sound like me at all" and 10 means "This sounds exactly like me." Students will choose a number between 1 and 10 to help describe the degree to which each way of learning sounds like themselves.

3. Assure students that there is no wrong or right answer and that they are just giving an estimate. Once they have estimated a number between one and ten, they will shade the bar graph to indicate the number they have chosen. Read one set of descriptors at a time and then pause to give students enough time to shade each column of the graph.

4. You may wish to model an example on an overhead as you go.

Analytical

   ♦ You prefer instructions to be step-by-step.
   ♦ You enjoy analyzing and solving problems.
   ♦ You enjoy playing games and doing puzzles that involve logic and strategy.
   ♦ You prefer questions that have a single, correct answer.
   ♦ You like to work in an organized environment.
   ♦ Rate yourself from 1 to 10.

Practical

   ♦ You prefer having real-life examples rather than examples that are created.
   ♦ You like handing objects when you learn.
   ♦ You would rather do experiments than read about them.
   ♦ You prefer questions that allow for practical applications and explanations.
   ♦ You are good at adapting to new situations.
   ♦ Rate yourself from 1 to 10.

Creative

   ♦ You prefer making your own connections between ideas rather than having them given to you.
   ♦ You prefer open-ended questions with no "correct" solution.
   ♦ You enjoy activities and tasks that are novel.
   ♦ You enjoy inventing and imagining new things.
   ♦ You prefer working in an informal, less structured, more flexible environment.
   ♦ Rate yourself from 1 to 10.

Triarchic Intelligences Graph

Name_____

Analytical	**Practical**	**Creative**

Blackline Master 6:
Parent-Completed Student Learning Preferences Inventory

Dear Parents,

The purpose of this inventory is to give a clear picture of some of your child's learning preferences so that we can capitalize on them over the course of the school year.

Thank you for completing this survey. Please return to school by _____.

Yours truly,

_____

What kinds of activities does your child gravitate toward? Check all that apply:

- ❑ Verbal
- ❑ Music
- ❑ Activities in Nature
- ❑ Working Alone

- ❑ Logical/Mathematical
- ❑ Physical Activities
- ❑ Puzzles/Mazes/Drawing
- ❑ Working with Others

1. What are your child's favorite subjects in school?

2. What subjects are your child's least favorite?

3. What are your child's interests outside of school?

5. When your child has free time, what does he or she choose to do?

6. What kinds of careers has your child expressed an interest in?

8. Describe how your child learns best (in a quiet place, with others, talking, etc.)

9. What else can you tell me about the way your child learns best?

10. What two words best describe how your child learns?

Blackline Master 7:
Intelligence Preferences—Parent Questionnaire

Child's name _____ Parent's name _____

I am gathering information about your child's natural talents and strengths. Please complete the following questionnaire and return by _____. Thank you for your input!

1. What are your child's favorite activities in school?

2. What are your child's hobbies and interests after school?

3. Check any of the activities below that your child particularly enjoys:
   - ☐ Reading (including newspapers, magazines, comics)
   - ☐ Writing (e.g., fiction or nonfiction, lists, diaries)
   - ☐ Drama (e.g., plays, magic shows, puppets, make believe, dress up)
   - ☐ Art (e.g., drawing, painting, doodling, modeling, crafts)
   - ☐ Music (e.g., remembers songs easily, listening to music, playing an instrument)
   - ☐ Math (calculating, logic puzzles, strategy games)
   - ☐ Movement (e.g., sports, working with hands, dancing)
   - ☐ Working or playing alone
   - ☐ Socializing, teamwork
   - ☐ Outdoor activities/nature
4. List other strengths or interests that aren't on the list above.

5. What is your child's favorite way to learn about new things?

6. Other comments that may be helpful in getting to know your child:

Blackline Master 8:
Visual

Blackline Master 9:
Auditory

Blackline Master 10:
Kinesthetic

Blackline Master 11:
Verbal/Linguistic

Blackline Master 12:
Logical/Mathematical

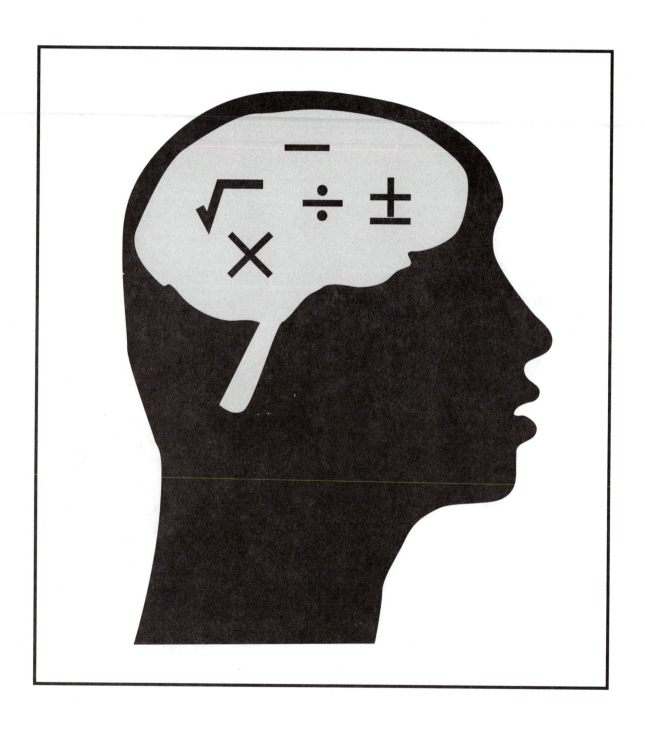

Blackline Master 13:
Musical/Rhythmic

Blackline Master 14:
Visual/Spatial

Blackline Master 15:
Body/Kinesthetic

Blackline Master 16:
Naturalist

Blackline Master 17: Interpersonal

Blackline Master 18:
Intrapersonal

Blackline Master 19:
Analytical

Blackline Master 20:
Practical

Blackline Master 21:
Creative

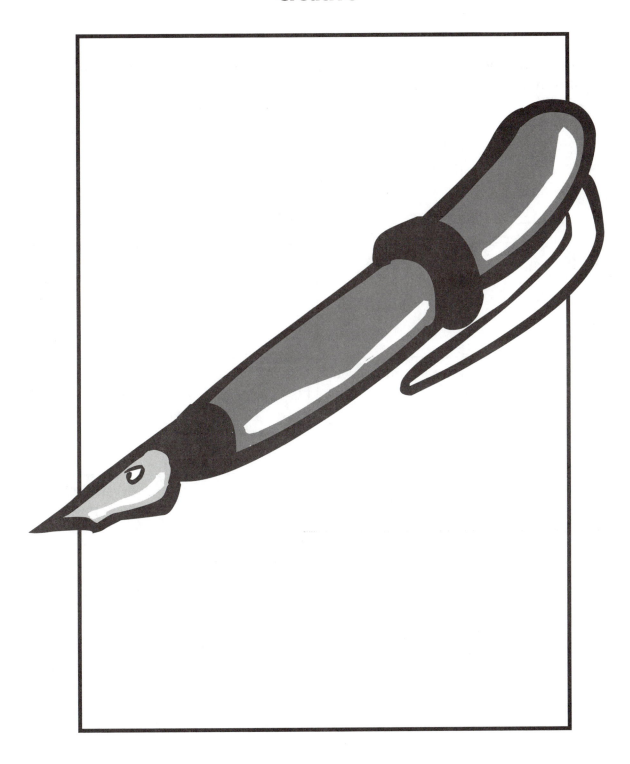

Blackline Master 22:
Learning Preferences People Search

Name: _____

Move around the classroom and have classmates sign their names in one of the squares that describes them.

Likes to draw	Remembers math facts	Plays a sport	Enjoys reading
Can remember a poem	Keeps a diary	Enjoys working in groups	Likes plants and animals
Likes doing crafts	Plays an instrument	Likes solving problems	Can interpret a graph
Enjoys being outside	Enjoys working alone	Can read a map	Enjoys taking things apart and putting things together
Likes to write	Enjoys jigsaw puzzles	Enjoys listening to music	Enjoys helping others

Blackline Master 23:
How I Use My
Visual Auditory Kinesthetic Preferences

In each square, draw or write words to represent all of the ways that you use each intelligence. Put a check mark beside the intelligence that you believe to be your strongest. Put a star beside the one you would most like to develop this year.

Visual	
Auditory	
Kinesthetic	

Blackline Master 24:
How I Use My Multiple Intelligences

In each space, draw or write words to represent all of the ways that you use each intelligence. Put a check mark beside the intelligences that you believe to be your strongest. Put a star beside the one you would most like to develop this year.

Verbal/ Linguistic	
Logical/ Mathematical	
Musical/ Rhythmic	
Visual/ Spatial	
Body/ Kinesthetic	
Naturalist	
Interpersonal	
Intrapersonal	

Blackline Master 25:
How I Use My Triarchic Intelligences

In each square, draw or write words to represent all of the ways you that you use each intelligence. Put a check mark beside the intelligence that you believe to be your strongest. Put a star beside the one you would most like to develop this year.

Analytical	
Practical	
Creative	

Blackline Master 26:
Learning Preferences Quilt Square

Blackline Master 27:
Learning Preferences Interviews

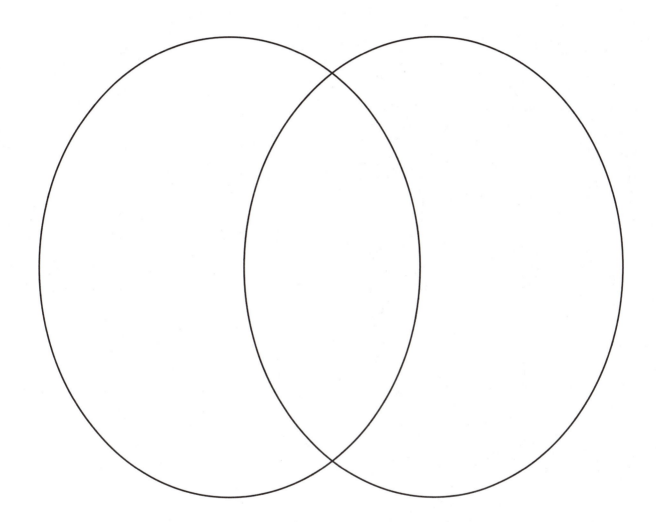

Blackline Master 28:
Triple Venn Learning Preferences Interviews

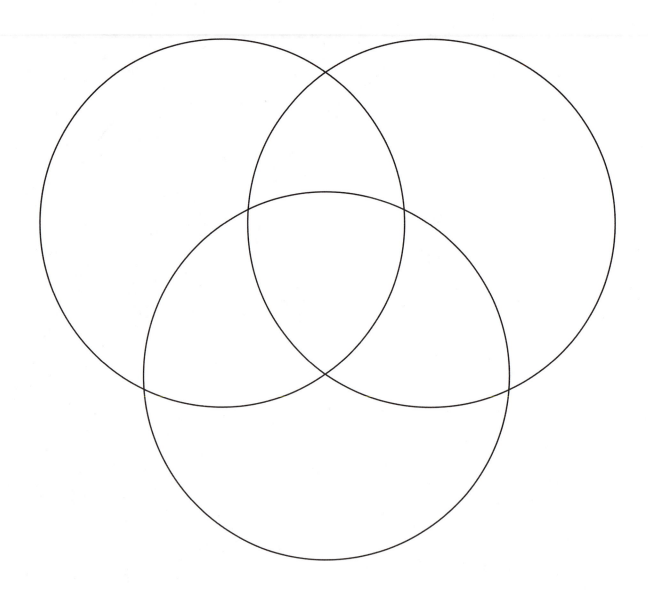

Blackline Master 29:
Visual Auditory Kinesthetic Group Graph

Group names_____

Visual	**Auditory**	**Kinesthetic**

Blackline Master 30: Multiple Intelligences Group Graph

Group Names _____

Verbal/ Linguistic	Logical/ Mathematical	Musical/ Rhythmic	Visual/ Spatial	Body/ Kinesthetic	Naturalist	Interpersonal	Intrapersonal

Blackline Master 31:
Triarchic Group Graph

Group names_____

Analytical	**Practical**	**Creative**

Blackline Master 32:
Student Profile Sheet

Student name: _____ Grade: _____

Readiness
Circle the descriptor most applicable:

Reading	Below Grade Level	At Grade Level	Above Grade Level
Writing	Below Grade Level	At Grade Level	Above Grade Level
Math	Below Grade Level	At Grade Level	Above Grade Level
Science	Below Grade Level	At Grade Level	Above Grade Level
Social Studies	Below Grade Level	At Grade Level	Above Grade Level

Learning Preferences
Circle as many as are applicable:

Sternberg:

Analytical	Practical	Creative

Gardner:

Verbal/ Linguistic	Logical/ Mathematical	Visual/ Spatial	Body/ Kinesthetic
Naturalist	Musical/ Rhythmic	Interpersonal	Intrapersonal

Visual Auditory Kinesthetic:

Visual	Auditory	Kinesthetic

Interests:

Other (group/individual orientation, quiet/noisy, parent observations, etc.):

Blackline Master 33:
Visual Auditory Kinesthetic Classroom Tracking Form

Check all of the intelligences strengths that apply to each student in the corresponding columns.

Student Name	Visual	Auditory	Kinesthetic
Classroom Preference Totals			

Blackline Master 34:
Multiple Intelligences Classroom Tracking Form

Check all of the intelligences strengths that apply to each student in the correspond-ing columns.

Student Name	V/L	L/M	M/R	V/S	B/K	N	Inter	Intra
Classroom Preference Totals								

Blackline Master 35:
Triarchic Classroom Tracking Form

Check all of the intelligences strengths that apply to each student in the corresponding columns.

Student Name	Analytical	Practical	Creative
Classroom Preference Totals			

Blackline Master 36:
Teacher Learning Preferences Self-Reflection

This self-reflection is designed to help you think about your own learning strengths, how they have changed over time, and what the implications are for teaching and learning with your students.

1. My learning strengths are:

2. My intelligences have developed over the years in the following ways:

3. The ways my own preferences affect my teaching are:

4. Intelligences I want to more consciously incorporate:

Blackline Master 37:
KUDos Quick Reference

Before we can effectively differentiate, we must be able to articulate what the outcomes will be. We must be clear on what we want students to **know, understand,** and **be able to do**.

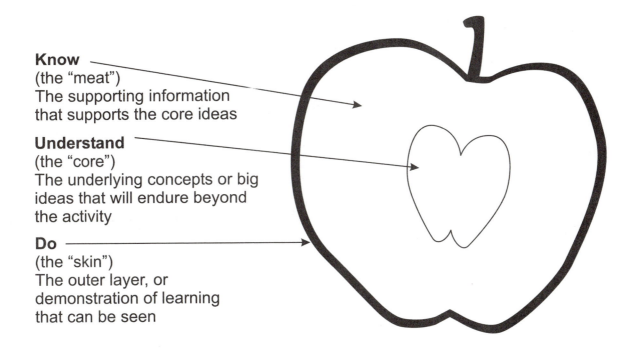

Know
(the "meat")
The supporting information
that supports the core ideas

Understand
(the "core")
The underlying concepts or big
ideas that will endure beyond
the activity

Do
(the "skin")
The outer layer, or
demonstration of learning
that can be seen

Blackline Master 38:
Steps to Create a Choice Board

1. Use curriculum documents to determine what you want the students to know, understand, and be able to do (KUDos).

2. Brainstorm a variety of tasks based on what you know about the learning preferences of your students.

3. Eliminate tasks that will not lead the students to KUDos.

4. Decide on the structure of your board. Will you create a tic-tac-toe, a list of choices, or something else?

5. Choose the activities from your brainstormed list and place them on the choice board.

6. Determine how student work will be shared and assessed.

Blackline Master 39:
Steps to Create a RAFT Project

1. Use curriculum documents to determine what you want the students to know, understand, and be able to do (KUDos).

2. Brainstorm a variety of projects based on what you know about the learning preferences of your students (these will become the formats).

3. Brainstorm roles, audiences, and topics for each format.

4. Eliminate ideas that will not lead the students to KUDos.

5. Place the roles, audience formats, and topics into the RAFT.

6. Determine how student work will be shared and assessed.

Blackline Master 40:
Visual Auditory Kinesthetic Cube

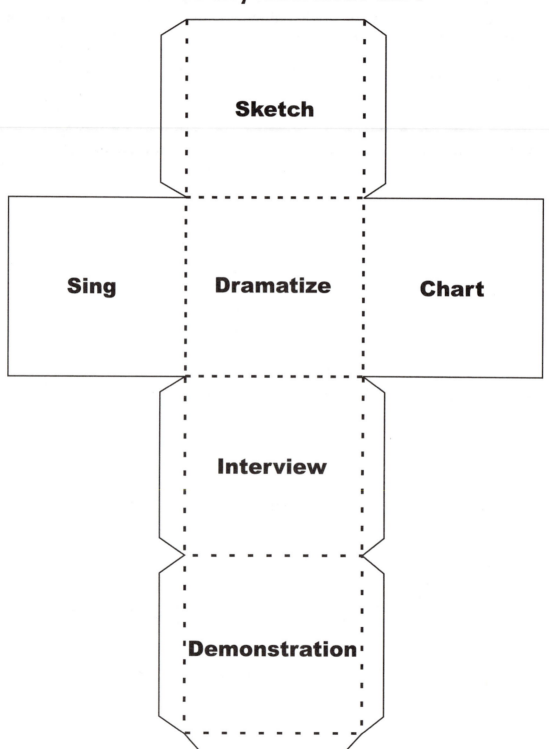

Blackline Master 41:
Multiple Intelligences Cube

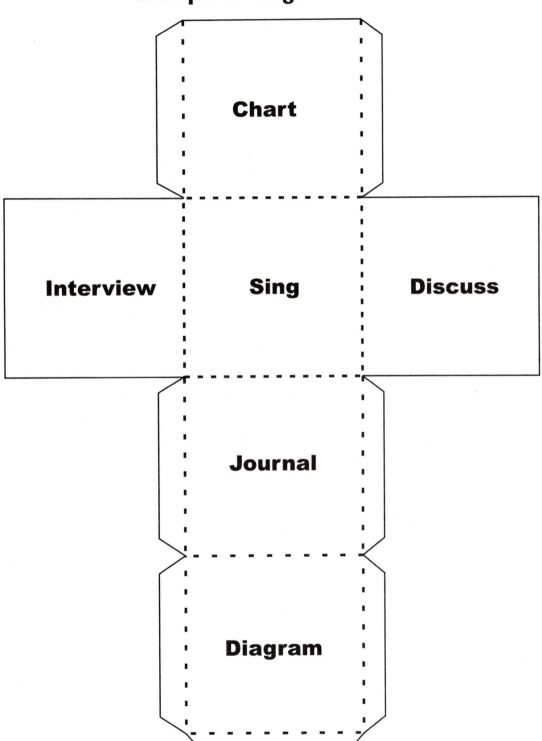

Blackline Master 42:
Triarchic Cube

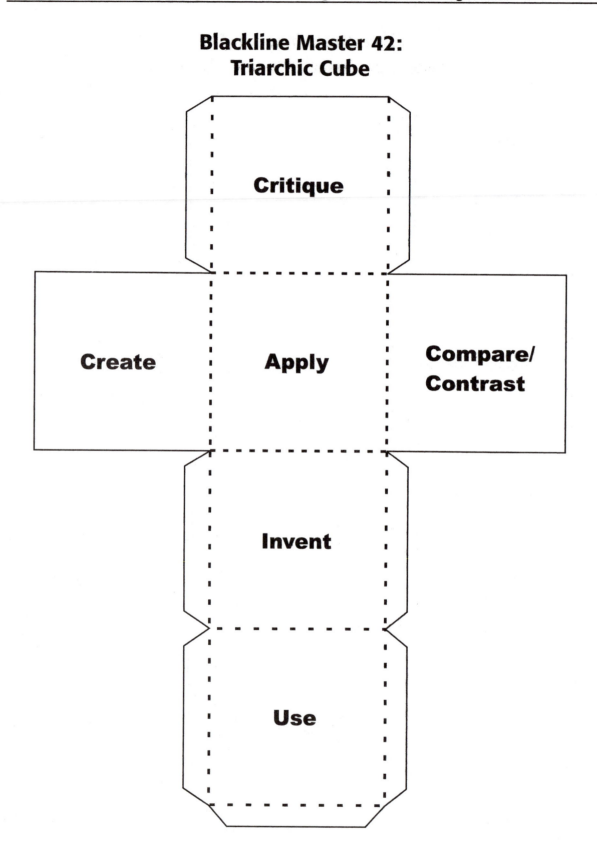

Critique

Create   Apply   Compare/Contrast

Invent

Use

Blackline Master 43:
Blank Cube

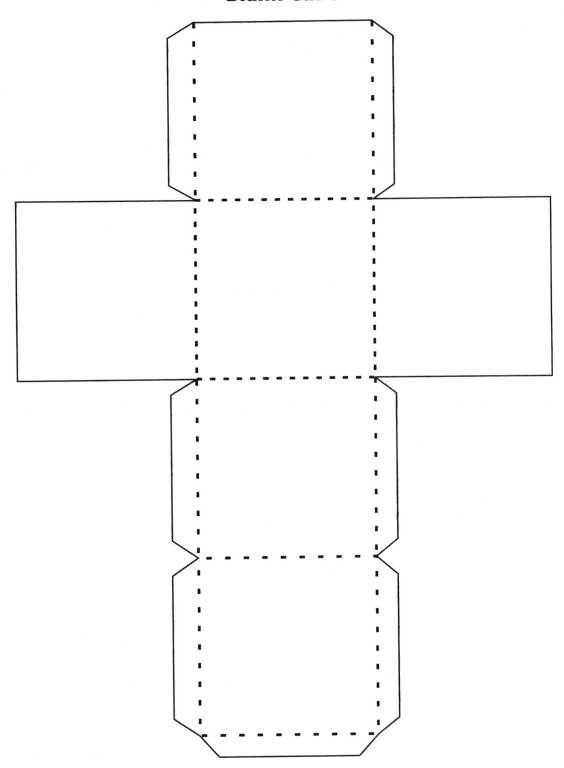

Blackline Master 44:
Steps to Create a Cubing Project

1. Use curriculum documents to determine what you want the students to know, understand, and be able to do (KUDos).

2. Brainstorm a variety of tasks based on what you know about the learning preferences of your students.

3. Eliminate tasks that will not lead the students to KUDos.

4. Choose the best six activities, so that there is one for each face of the cube.

5. Create the cube(s).

6. Determine how student work will be shared and assessed.

Blackline Master 45:
Steps to Create a Learning Contract

1. Use curriculum documents to determine what you want the students to know, understand, and be able to do (KUDos).

2. Brainstorm a variety of tasks based on what you know about the learning preferences of your students.

3. Eliminate tasks that will not lead the students to KUDos.

4. Choose activities that will be included in the learning contract.

5. Determine how many tasks students will do.

6. Decide on a reasonable timeline to complete the tasks.

7. Determine in what way and how often you will check in with students during their contract work. Make this explicit in the contract.

8. Outline how students will ask for help, if needed.

9. List the resources that students are able to use and how they should be cited.

10. Write up the contract in a businesslike manner. Be sure to include places for dates and signatures.

11. Determine how student work will be shared and assessed. Include this information with the contract. If rubrics or scoring guides are to be used, include them as well.

Blackline Master 46:
Steps to Create a WebQuest

1. Use curriculum documents to determine what you want the students to know, understand, and be able to do (KUDos).

2. Brainstorm a variety of tasks based on what you know about the learning preferences of your students.

3. Eliminate tasks that will not lead the students to KUDos.

4. Search for web sites that are of an appropriate reading level and contain information that students will need.

5. Design on an introduction or "hook" that will engage students in the task.

6. Describe the task(s) that the students will complete during the WebQuest.

7. Write step-by-step instructions for the WebQuest process and add the links students will use to find information.

8. Determine how student work will be assessed.

9. Decide on how student work will be shared.

Blackline Master 47:
Steps to Create a Lesson Differentiated by Learning Preference

1. Identify the subject and topic of study.

2. Use curriculum documents to determine what you want the students to know, understand, and be able to do (KUDos).

3. Decide on an activity structure that will allow students to choose a task that interests them (e.g., choice board, RAFT, cubing activity, learning contract, WebQuest, etc.).

4. Brainstorm a variety of tasks based on what you know about the learning preferences of your students.

5. Eliminate tasks that will not lead the students to KUDos.

6. Choose the activities that will be the most engaging for your students and best match their learning preferences.

7. Check to see that all students will reach the same KUDos, no matter which task(s) they complete.

8. Describe the learning activities in detail. Create student handouts, if appropriate.

9. Determine how student work will be assessed.

10. Decide how you will facilitate sharing and bring closure to the lesson.

Blackline Master 48:
Differentiating by Learning Preference—
Lesson Plan Template

Subject:	Topic:

Outcomes: As a result of this study, students should:

    Know:

    Understand:

    Be able to do:

Learning Preference Model

    ❑ Visual Auditory Kinesthetic
    ❑ Multiple Intelligences
    ❑ Triarchic
    ❑ Other

Activity Structure:

❑ Choice Board	❑ RAFT
❑ Cube	❑ Learning Contract
❑ WebQuest	❑ Other

Description of Learning Activities:

Assessment:

Closure/Sharing:

Blackline Master 49:
Visual Auditory Kinesthetic Project Ideas

Visual	Auditory	Kinesthetic
scrapbook	song	drama
brochure	speech	dance
video	audio recording	model
poster	group discussion	sculpt
collage	storytelling	construct
comic book	talk show	perform an experiment
mural	interview	pantomime
chart	rap	role play
map	nursery rhyme	creative movement
PowerPoint	debate	puppet show
photographs	editorial	charades
display	readers theater	demonstration
graph	radio show	group game
flow chart	audio journal	scavenger hunt
diagram	jokes/riddles	craft
mind map	public service announcement	tableau

Blackline Master 50:
Multiple Intelligences Project Ideas

Verbal/ Linguistic	Logical/ Mathematical	Visual/ Spatial	Body/ Kinesthetic
radio program	real-world problem	model	model
diary	write a new law	slide show	play
mock interview	timeline	video	game
dictionary	chart	children's book	demonstration
press conference	spreadsheet	painting	mime
video	graph	digital photos	construct
debate	fact file	diagram	experiment
list	database	picture dictionary	role play

Musical/ Rhythmic	Naturalist	Interpersonal	Intrapersonal
song lyrics	recycled art	game	reflection
rap	natural collections	discussion group	diary
poem	observation	meeting	blog
melody	taxonomy	service project	advice column
song collection	WebQuest	teach	autobiography
background music	explore	feedback	goal setting
commercial jingle	forecast	e-mail	philosophy
rhythm	categorize	readers theater	monologue

Blackline Master 51:
Triarchic Intelligences Project Ideas

Analytical	Practical	Creative
chart	scenario	picture
graphic organizer	role play	doodle
timeline	WebQuest	song
Venn diagram	job shadowing	invention
t-chart	dialog	riddles
patterns	newscast	commercial
sequencing	letter to the editor	mime
classifying	flyer	sculpture
definitions	scenario	play
cause/effect	role play	drama
code	demonstration	speech
graph	experiment	mural
database	real-world problem	fairy tale
blueprints	survey	monologue
newspaper	field trip	bumper sticker
fact file	petition	travelogue

Blackline Master 52:
Surprising but True!

Not many successful people find their success without great effort. Consider the following:

Albert Einstein was unable to speak fluently at age nine.

Charles Shultz, creator of the Peanuts cartoon strip, had his drawings for his high school rejected.

Bill Gates of Microsoft failed with his first business idea, a device that could record traffic data.

Your assignment is to choose a famous person or someone you know who had to work hard and overcome roadblocks before they became successful. You can choose to share your project in one of the following ways:

- ◆ Brochure
- ◆ Public Service Announcement
- ◆ Song
- ◆ Poem (oral or written)
- ◆ Chart
- ◆ Talk show
- ◆ Mind map
- ◆ Diary/blog

As you work on your project, ensure it includes the following information:

- ☐ A description of why the person is well known.
- ☐ A description of the roadblocks they experienced before they found success.
- ☐ A quote
- ☐ A description of how the person's willingness to persist through hard times will inspire you to keep trying when you encounter difficulty.

Your project will be due on _____. Good luck and have fun!

Blackline Master 53:
Children's Literature to Support a Climate for Differentiated Instruction

All the Colors of the Earth by Sheila Hamanaka

Amazing Grace by Mary Hoffman

Being Friends by Karen Beaumont

Chrysanthemum by Kevin Henkes

A Color of His Own by Leo Lionni

Crow Boy by Taro Yashima

Do You Want to Be My Friend? by Eric Carle

The Dot by Peter Reynolds

Frederick by Leo Lionni

Frog and Toad Are Friends by Arnold Lobel

Giraffes Can't Dance by Gilles Andrae

I Like Me by Nancy Carlson

Important Book by Margaret Wise Brown

Incredible Me by Kathi Appelt

Ira Sleeps Over by Bernard Waber

Ish by Peter Reynolds

Just Because I Am: A Child's Book of Affirmation by Lauren Murphy Payne

The Keeping Quilt by Patricia Polacco

Leo, the Late Bloomer by Robert Kraus

Lilly's Purple Plastic Purse by Kevin Henkes

The Little Engine that Could by Watty Piper, George Hauman, and Doris Hauman

The Mixed-Up Chameleon by Eric Carle

My Best Friend by Pat Hutchins

No Two Snowflakes by Shere Fitch

Oh, the Places You'll Go! by Dr. Seuss

People by Peter Spier

The Rainbow Fish by Marcus Pfister

Rainbow Fish to the Rescue by Marcus Pfister

A Rainbow of Friends by P. K. Hallinan

Seven Blind Mice by Ed Young

Some Dogs Do by Jez Alborough

Someday by Alison McGhee

Stand Tall, Molly Lou Melon by Patty Lovell

Super-Completely and Totally the Messiest by Judith Viorst

The Skin You Live In by Michael Tyler

The Table Where Rich People Sit by Byrd Baylor

Unique Monique by Maria Rousaki

Wanda and the Wild Hair by Barbara Azore

We All Sing with the Same Voice by Philip Miller

We Are All Related—A Celebration of Our Cultural Heritage by the students of
  G. T. Cunningham Elementary School

We Can Be Friends by Denise Jordan

Whoever You Are by Mem Fox

Blackline Master 54: 25 Active Learning Ideas

1	**Card Sort**	The teacher (or students) prepares two sets of cards. One set should contain corresponding definitions. Students work in teams to find matches. It can be helpful if the terms and definitions sets are done on two different colors of paper.
2	**Carousel Brainstorming**	The teacher posts charts on the wall with key questions or ideas at the top. Groups are formed and one person scribes for the group and adds to the chart as they brainstorm. Groups move to a new chart, read other groups' responses, and add to the chart. Teams may use a different color of felt pen.
3	**Find the Expert**	The teacher polls the class to see which students have special knowledge to share on a topic. Those students become the experts and stand in different parts of the room. The remaining students are divided evenly into groups and sit around an expert. They listen as the student explains his or her special understanding of the topic and then ask questions of him or her. They could also take notes, if appropriate. Groups rotate around the room until they have had an opportunity to hear from each expert.
4	**Four Corners**	The teacher poses a question and gives four potential responses and points to a corner for each one (the teacher might want to post a visual cue in each corner in advance). Students move to their chosen corner and discuss the topic with those who also chose that corner. The students then come together for a whole-class discussion.
5	**Gallery Walk with Docent**	After teams have generated ideas on a topic using a piece of chart paper, they appoint a "docent" to stay with their work. Teams rotate around, examining other team's ideas and asking questions of the docent. Teams then meet together to discuss and add to their information so that the docent also can learn from other teams.
6	**Graffiti**	Groups receive a large piece of paper and felt pens of different colors. Students generate ideas and write them quickly as if they were creating graffiti on a wall. Groups can move to other papers carousel style and discuss or add to the ideas of other groups, if desired.
7	**Human Continuum**	The teacher poses a question or problem and students line up according to their opinion on the answer.
8	**Inside/Outside Circle**	The teacher divides class in half. One group forms a circle and then turns to face outward. Those from the remaining group find one person in the circle to stand opposite (so there are two circles of people facing each other). Information can be shared and reviewed, and the outer circle can move easily (e.g., The teacher could call, "Outside circle people, move three places to the right.") to generate more responses or discuss new information.
9	**Jigsaw**	"Home groups" (using small number of students) are formed. Each home group member is assigned a number. Students move to an "expert group" containing others who have the same number (e.g., All "number ones" together). They read a short section of information from a textbook (or other material) independently and then work together to decide what is important. After discussion in these "expert groups" everyone returns to the "home group," and each expert teaches his or her portion of the material.
10	**Line Up**	Students line up according to a prompt by the teacher. Examples might be to line up by house number, birthday, etc. They can then discuss with an elbow partner (someone with whom they can touch elbows without changing place in the line) or in a small group.
11	**Most Stay, One Strays**	Students work in a team to solve a problem. While they work, they send one member to "stray" to other groups to bring new ideas back to the team.

Blackline Master 54: 25 Active Learning Ideas (Continues)

12	Numbered Heads Together	Students sit in groups and each group member is given a number. The teacher poses a problem, and all four students discuss so that each is able to respond to the question. The teacher calls a number and that student is responsible for sharing for the group.
13	Pass a Problem	The teacher creates problems for teams to solve and writes them on or attaches them to envelopes. Teams read the problems, place their solutions in the envelope, and then exchange with another team to check their solution and to determine whether they solved the problem correctly (or in a different way).
14	Round-Robin Brainstorming	The class is divided into small groups with one person appointed as the recorder. A question is posed, and students are given time to think about and write their answers individually. Next, members of the team share responses with one another, round-robin style. The recorder writes down the ideas of the group members.
15	Say and Switch	Partners take turns responding to a topic given by the teacher at signaled times. The times will be unpredictable and the person listening must pick up from their partner's train of thought before adding new ideas.
16	Send a Question	Students work in teams to write a review question on a card and ask other teams to solve it. The team that writes the question determines whether they have come up with a good solution.
17	Talking Chips	Students are given a certain number of chips. Each time they talk, they must submit a chip, but once their chips are gone they may no longer talk. Students should try to use all their chips.
18	ThinkPad Brainstorming	Students individually brainstorm and write down their answers on a pad of scrap paper. Once they are all done, they are to share their information with a partner or a team.
19	Think/Pair/Share	First, individuals think silently about a question posed by the teacher. Student pair up and exchange thoughts. Finally, the pairs share their responses with the whole class.
20	Think/Ink/ Pair/Share	This strategy uses same process as think/pair/share, except that after students have time to think, they are asked to "ink" or write their ideas on paper before they share.
21	Think/Pair/ Square	This is the same process as think/pair/share, except that partners share with another set of partners before the whole-class discussion.
22	Three-minute Pause	The teacher stops any time during a class discussion, story, video, or other learning experience and gives partners or teams three minutes to review what has been said and to ask clarifying questions.
23	Three-Step Interview	Partners interview each other about themselves or a subject-specific topic. They then find another team and form a group of four. Each person shares what they learned from the original partner.
24	Two Facts and a Fib	Students or the teacher write down two facts and one idea that is not true. Each team tries to identify which is which. This can be done using personal experiences or subject-related material.
25	Visible Quiz	The teacher poses questions with multiple-choice responses and students sit in teams and discuss the responses. When the teacher asks, they hold up their answers and may be called on to explain their team's reasoning.

Blackline Master 55:
Visual Auditory Kinesthetic Intelligences Planner

Instructions: Copy and use as a tool to track how often you are using each intelligence in your classroom.

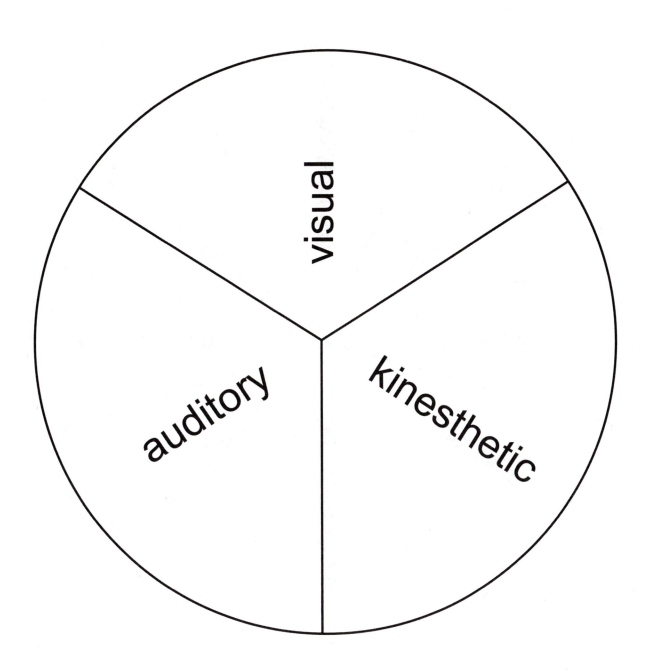

Blackline Master 56:
Multiple Intelligences Planner

Instructions: Copy and use as a tool to track how often you are using each intelligence in your classroom.

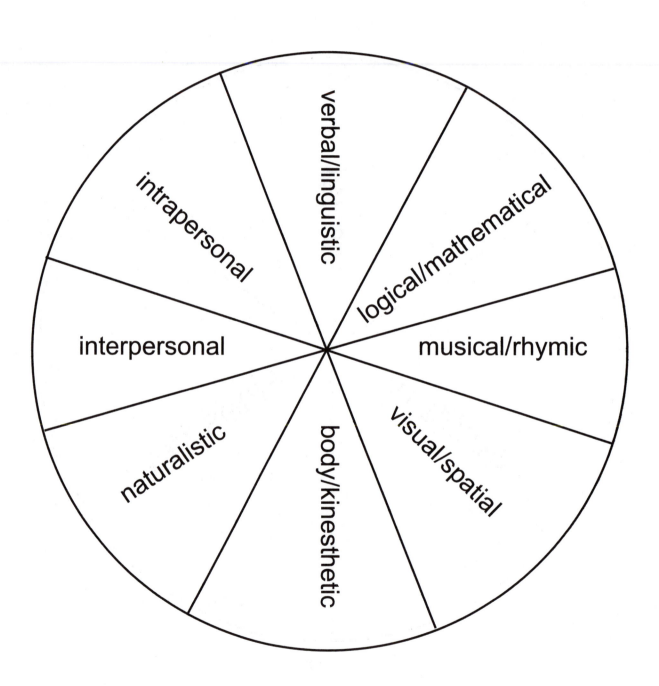

Blackline Master 57:
Triarchic Intelligences Planner

Instructions: Copy and use as a tool to track how often you are using each intelligence in your classroom.

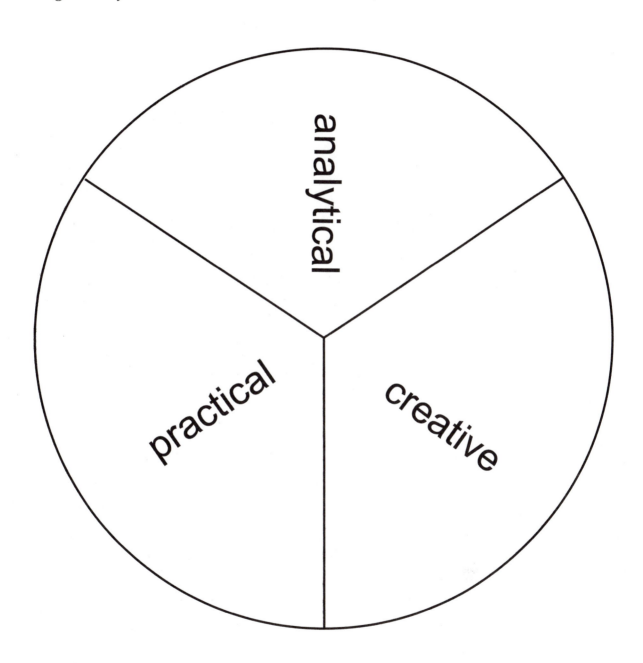

References

Armstrong, T. (2000). *Multiple intelligences in the classroom* (2nd ed.). Alexandria, VA: Association for Supervision and Curriculum Development.

Brendtro, L. K., Brokenleg, M., & Van Bockern, S. (2002). *Reclaiming youth at risk: Our hope for the future* (Rev. ed.) Bloomington, IN: Solution Tree.

Chapman C., & King, R. (2005). *Differentiated assessment strategies: One tool doesn't fit all.* Thousand Oaks, CA: Corwin Press.

Collins, M. A., & Amabile, T. M. (1999). Motivation and creativity. In R. J. Sternberg (Ed.), *Handbook of creativity*, (pp. 297–312). Cambridge, UK: Cambridge University Press.

Dodge, B. (1997). Some thoughts about WebQuests. Retrieved April 15, 2004, from http://edweb.sdsu.edu/courses/edtec596/about_webquests.html.

Dunn, R. (1984). Learning style: State of the science. *Theory into Practice, 23*(1), 10–19.

Gardner, H. (1983). *Frames of mind: The theory of multiple intelligences.* New York: Basic Books.

Gardner, H. (1999). *Intelligence reframed: Multiple intelligences for the 21st century.* New York: Basic Books.

Gardner, H., & Moran, S. (2006). The science of multiple intelligences: A response to Lynn Waterhouse. *Educational Psychologist, 41*(4), 227–232.

Geimer, M., Getz, J., Pochert, T., & Pullam, K. (2000). *Improving student achievement in language arts through implementation of multiple intelligences strategies.* Chicago: Saint Xavier University. (ERIC Document Reproduction Service No. ED444185)

Gens, P., Provance, J., VanDuyne, K., & Zimmerman, K. (1998). *The effects of integrating a multiple intelligence based language arts curriculum on reading comprehension of first and second grade students.* Chicago: Saint Xavier University. (ERIC Document Reproduction Service No. ED420840)

Greenhawk, J. (1997). Multiple intelligences meet standards. *Educational Leadership, 55*(1), 62–64.

Gregorc, A. (1982). *Inside styles: Beyond the basics.* Columbia, CT: Gregorc Associates.

Heacox, D. (2002). Differentiating instruction in the regular classroom: How to reach and teach all learners, grades 3–12. Minneapolis, MN: Free Spirit Publishing.

Jung, C. (1927). *The theory of psychological type.* Princeton, NJ: Princeton University Press.

Kolb, D. A. (1976). *Learning styles inventory: Technical manual.* Boston: McBer and Co.

Kornhaber, M., Fierros, E., & Veenema, S. (2004). *Multiple intelligences: Best ideas from research and practice.* Boston: Allyn & Bacon.

Kuzniewski, R, Sanders, M., Smith, G. S., Swanson, S., & Urich, C. (1998). *Using multiple intelligences to increase reading comprehension in English and math.* (Rep. No. CS-O1 3-228). Chicago: Saint Xavier University. (ERIC Document Reproduction Service No. ED420839)

Mattingly, D., Prislin, R., McKenzie, T., Rodriguez, J., & Kayzar, B. (2002). Evaluating evaluations: The case of parent involvement programs. *Review of Educational Research, 72*(4), 549–576.

McCarthy, B. (1979). *The 4MAT system: Teaching to learning styles with left/right mode techniques.* Oak Brook, IL: Excel.

McMahon, S. D., Rose, D. S., & Parks, M. (2004). Multiple intelligences and reading achievement: An examination of the Teele Inventory of Multiple Intelligences. *Journal of Experimental Education, 73*(1), 41–52.

Mettetal, G., Jordan, C., & Harper, S. (1997). Attitudes toward a multiple intelligences curriculum. *Journal of Educational Research, 91(2), 115–122.*

Nahagawa, K. (2000). Unthreading the ties that bind: Questioning the discourse of parent involvement. *Educational Policy, 14*(4), 443–472.

Sadler-Smith, E. (1996). Learning styles and instructional design. *Innovations in Education and Training International, 33,* 185–193.

Silver, H., Strong, R., & Perini, M. (1997). Integrating learning styles and multiple intelligences. *Educational Leadership, 55*(1), 22–27.

Smith, P., & Dalton, J. (2005). *Getting to grips with learning styles.* Adelaide, Australia: National Centre for Vocational Educational Research.

Sparks, R. L., & Castro, O. (2006). Learning styles—Making too many "wrong mistakes": A response to Castro and Peck. *Foreign Language Annals, 39*(3), 520–535.

Sternberg, R. (2000). Patterns of giftedness: A triarchic analysis. *Roeper Review, 22*(4), 231–235.

Sternberg, R. J., & Grigorenko, E. L. (2004). Successful intelligence in the classroom. *Theory into Practice, 43*(4), 274–280

Sternberg, R. J., & Zhang, L. (2005). Styles of thinking as a basis of differentiated instruction. *Theory into Practice, 44*(3), 245–253.

Teele, S. (1995). *The multiple intelligences school: A place for all students to succeed.* Redlands, CA: Citrograph.

Teele, S. (1999). *Rainbows of intelligence: Exploring how students learn.* Redlands, CA: Citrograph.

Tomlinson, C.A. (2001). *How to differentiate instruction in mixed-ability classrooms.* Alexandria VA: Association for Supervision and Curriculum Development.

Tomlinson, C. A. (2004). Research evidence for differentiation. *School Administrator, 61*(7), 30.

Tomlinson, C. A., & Allan, S. D. (2000). *Leadership for differentiating schools and classrooms.* Alexandria, VA: Association for Supervision and Curriculum Development.

Van Klaveren, K., Buckland, T., Williamson, J. L., Kunselman, M. M., Wiklinson, J., & Cunningham, S. (2002). How do your students learn? *Science Scope, 25*(7), 24.

Williamson, M. F., & Watson, R. L. (2007). Learning styles research: Understanding how teaching should be impacted by the way learners learn. Part III: Understanding how learners' personality styles impact learning. *Christian Education Journal, 4*(1), 62–77.

Wormeli, R. (2005). Busting myths about differentiated instruction. *Principal Leadership, 5*(7), 28–33.

Wormeli, R. (2006). *Fair isn't always equal: Assessing and grading in the differentiated classroom.* Portland, ME: Stenhouse.